MINNESOTA
Monuments, Festivals & Historic Sites
MUSEUMS

ANNE ARTHUR

I want to thank my family for their support and help with this book.

Book and cover design by Jonathan Norberg
Published by Adventure Publications, Inc.
820 Cleveland St. S
Cambridge, MN 55008
1-800-678-7006

ISBN 1-59193-014-6

PREFACE

This book is a collection of historic sites, museums and festivals. It is intended as a guide for those who wish to find unique places to visit around the state. Hopefully, it will be a guide not only for the tourist but also for local residents. I have endeavored to find as many of the museums and sites as possible. I'm sure that I have not found every last one! If your favorite museum or festival is not listed, please send me a letter in care of Adventure Publications, 820 Cleveland St. S., Cambridge, MN 55008 and we'll try to include it in a future edition.

For a state that is relatively young, history abounds in Minnesota. Indian burial mounds, tributes to the voyageurs and fur traders that traveled along our lakes and rivers, the remains of homes constructed by early settlers and forts left by soldiers are among the many historic sites around the state. In particular, the Dakota Conflict of 1862 is remembered in many locations along the Minnesota River. Minnesotans are proud of their history and have put it on display. Another wonderful resource for information on Minnesota's historical sites is a website www.exploreminnesota.com which is maintained by the Minnesota Department of Tourism. Have fun exploring our state and our history!

How to Use this Book

This book is organized into six Minnesota regions. Within each region, there is a list of museums and a list of festivals. Locate the largest city you are in or near and you'll find the museums and festivals that are within about an hour's drive of that city. Each listing includes a description, hours of operation and other details. There are also four indexes in the back of the book which you'll find helpful. The first is by city (the actual city the museum is in), the second is by county, the third is by interest and the fourth lists the attractions alphabetically. If, for example, you know the name of a museum you wish to locate, use the alphabetical index. If you're interested in railroad history, check the attraction by interest index. The county and city indexes are helpful when you want to find a museum or festival near your vacation destination or your home.

CONTENTS

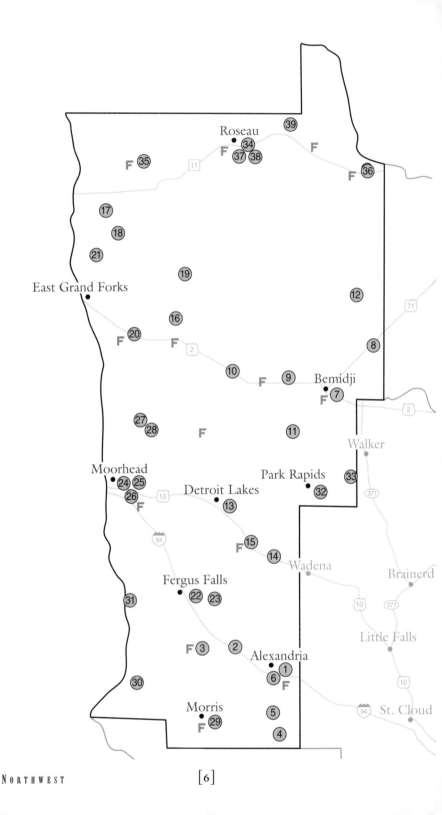

Roseau

F 35

17

18

21

East Grand Forks

19

16

F 20   F

10   F   9   Bemidji
F 7

27
28   F   11   Walker

Moorhead
24 25   Park Rapids   33
26   10   Detroit Lakes   32
F   13

94   15
14   Wadena   Brainerd

Fergus Falls
22 23

31

F 3   2   Alexandria
1
6
F

30

Morris   5
F 29
4

39

34
F 37 38   F
F 36

12   71

8

371

10   371

Little Falls

371   10

94   St. Cloud

NORTHWEST MINNESOTA

ATTRACTIONS WITHIN AN HOUR'S DRIVE OF:

(#) = historic sites   **F** = festivals

Listings in grey print are found in other sections but are within an hour's drive of the city.

DOUGLAS COUNTY HISTORICAL SOCIETY

① Description: This Historical Society is located in the historic home of Senator Knute Nelson. Knute Nelson immigrated to the US, eventually arriving in Alexandria in 1871. He went on to become governor in 1893 and then senator for 28 years. There is a statue of Knute Nelson in front of the Minnesota Capitol.

This turn-of-the-century home has been beautifully restored, and many of the original furnishings have remained. Visitors can take a guided tour of the house and of Douglas County, as well as use the public research center featuring a slide show program and a vintage clothing and uniform collection.

Seasons/Hours: 10 am–4 pm M–F; society hours: 8 am–5 pm; weekends by appointment

Cost: Tours: $2; use of research center: $7.50

Address: 1219 N Nokomis St, Alexandria, MN 56308

Phone/Fax: Ph: 320.762.0382; Fax: 320.762.9062

E-mail: historic@rea-alp.com

Website: www.rea-alp.com/~historic/

Directions: In Alexandria, take Hwy 29 N to N Nokomis St.

EVANSVILLE HISTORICAL FOUNDATION

② Description: The Evansville Historical Foundation maintains a Pioneer Village. Visitors can see the Johnson house containing antique items depicting the pioneer era, a red brick one-room schoolhouse, a log cabin home with furnishings, a town hall, a church, a root and fruit cellar, and a dugout home on the hillside covered with sod and wildflowers. Family files available for genealogical research.

Seasons/Hours: Apr–Oct: 11 am-3 pm M–F; or by appointment

Cost: Free

Address: 304 Gran St, PO Box 337, Evansville, MN 56326

Phone: 320.948.2010; if no answer, call 218.948.2863 or 218.948.2331

E-mail: ehf@gctel.com

Website: www.evansvillemn.net/EHF/evansville_historical_ foundation.htm

Directions: Exit I-94 N of Alexandria, S of Fergus Falls to Cty Rd 41/MN

Hwy 79 toward Elbow Lake and Evansville. Turn right on Cty Rd 41, which becomes Cty Rd 82. Make a sharp right on S Gran St.

GRANT COUNTY HISTORICAL SOCIETY

③ **Description:** The Grant County Historical Society will take visitors back through many different time periods, from prehistoric times to the 1900s and early pioneer life. Come and see the oldest ox cart, an early stagecoach, a rural schoolhouse and a furnished log cabin. To finish your visit, wander back to the 1900s on one small town's Main Street. Genealogical research available.

Seasons/Hours: Year-round: 10 am–12 pm & 1 pm–4 pm M–F; also open Sa in the summer

Cost: Admission: $2; research: $2 in person, $10 via phone, mail, etc.

Address: Hwy 79 E, Elbow Lake, MN 56531

Phone: 218.685.4864

Website: www.rootsweb.com/~mngrant/history.htm

Directions: From Hwy 59 and 79, go ½ block E on 79.

HISTORIC TERRACE MILL

④ **Description:** The Terrace Mill Foundation maintains the historic Terrace Mill District and it is home to a reconstructed 1870s log house, the Keystone Arch Bridge, an art gallery and the Historic Terrace Mill. Stroll the district and see how things looked in the late nineteenth and early twentieth centuries. Numerous events throughout the summer and fall.

Seasons/Hours: 12 pm–5 pm Su and W; 12 pm–9 pm Thu–Sa; closed M and T; other times by appointment

Address: Terrace Mill Foundation, 27165 Old Mill Pond Road, Terrace, MN 56334

Phone/Fax: Ph: 320.278.3728

E-mail: information@terracemill.org

Website: mywebpage.netscape.com/terracemill/

Directions: From I 94, take Alexandria-Glenwood exit S on Hwy 29 to Glenwood. At stoplight in Glenwood, cross Minnesota Avenue and continue S out of town on Hwy 104. Turn left at Terrace sign. Terrace Mill is at bottom of hill.

POPE COUNTY HISTORICAL SOCIETY

⑤ *Description:* Campus includes a genealogy library, exhibit galleries, 6 historic buildings and outdoor displays of agricultural and industrial equipment. Unique collection of Native American arts and crafts. Exhibits change regularly. Occasional special events throughout the year.

Seasons/Hours: Year-round: 10 am–5 pm T–Sa

Cost: Adults: $3, students 13-18: $1.50, children 12 & under: $.50

Address: 809 South Lakeshore Drive, Glenwood, MN 56334

Phone/Fax: Ph: 320.634.3283;

E-mail: pcmuseum@runestone.net

Directions: From Alexandria, S on Hwy 29 to Glenwood. Continue S to 809 South Hwy 104. Watch for sign on the left.

RUNESTONE MUSEUM

⑥ *Description:* The museum's centerpiece, the world-famous and controversial Kensington Runestone, is not the only piece to learn about. Other exhibits display Minnesota wildlife, Viking artifacts found in the area, firearms and accessories, and life of the Native Americans and pioneers in the nineteenth century.

Big Ole

Seasons/Hours: 2nd weekend of Oct–Mother's Day: 9 am–5 pm M–F; 9 am–3 pm Sa; summer hours: 9 am–5 pm M–F; 9 am–3 pm Sa; 11 am–4 pm Su

Cost: Adults: $5, senior citizens: $4, students: $3, children under 7: free; families: $12

Address: 206 Broadway, Alexandria, MN 56308

Phone/Fax: Ph: 320.763.3160; Fax: 320.763.9705

E-mail: bigole@rea-alp.com

Website: www.runestonemuseum.org

Directions: Next to the Big Ole statue in downtown Alexandria. Use Exit 103 off I-94.

Alexandria is home to Big Ole, a 28' tall, 4-ton Viking statue. He was built for the 1965 New York World's Fair to represent the area as the "Birthplace of America," as sited by the Kensington Runestone.

BELTRAMI COUNTY HISTORY CENTER

⑦ **Description:** This beautifully preserved Neoclassical style museum—listed on the National Register of Historic Places—is the last depot built in 1912 by James J. Hill, otherwise known as the "Empire Builder." The museum features "Voices & Visions of Beltrami County" which will evoke emotions as soldiers from the Civil War to Vietnam tell stories in their own words. History of the county can be discovered through the use of the research library's microfilm, some 100,000 photographs, 2,000 historical maps and other types of records available.

Seasons/Hours: Year-round: 10 am–5 pm M–Th; 10 am–4 pm F–Sa (Sa May–Oct only)

Cost: Adults: $3, students, seniors and children: $1.50; families and groups: $10; Beltrami County Historical Society Members: free

Address: 130 Minnesota Ave SW, Bemidji, MN 56601

Mailing Address: PO Box 683, Bemidji, MN 56619

Phone/Fax: Ph: 218.444.DEPO (3376); Fax: 218.444.3377

E-mail: depot@paulbunyan.net

Website: www.paulbunyan.net/users/depot

Directions: From Bemidji Ave turn W on 2nd Ave. Go 3 blocks and turn left across the railroad tracks.

CAMP RABIDEAU CCC CAMP

⑧ **Description:** Camp Rabideau Civilian Conservation Corps (CCC) Camp is a remnant of FDR's New Deal that gave young men around the country the opportunity to work and become educated. The men at this camp worked on projects such as tree planting, and the construction of fire towers and the Blackduck ranger station. They took classes such as typing and English, but also learned boxing and ping pong skills during their leisure time.

Built in 1935, this CCC camp is of the best preserved in the country and is now on the National Register of Historic Places.

There are interpretive signs, a picnic site, a nearby lake to fish and swim, and a 1-mile trail that runs through Camp Rabideau.

Seasons/Hours:	The grounds are open daily to drive through at any time. Contact the Forest Service for the buildings' hours.
Cost:	Free
Mailing Address:	HC 3 Box 95, Blackduck, MN 56630
Phone:	218.835.4291
E-mail:	mnipp@fs.fed.us
Website:	www.fs.fed.us/r9/chippewa/camp/camprabideau.htm
Directions:	From Blackduck, go 6 mi. S on Cty Rd 39.

CLEARWATER COUNTY HISTORICAL CENTER

⑨ *Description:*	The Historical Society maintains the historic Shevlin school grounds, on which is a 1911 brick schoolhouse where photos and artifacts can be found. The first log school in the county built in the 1880s, a log cabin from the 1890s and a 1936 Works Progress Administration (WPA) clapboard schoolhouse can all be found on the school grounds.
Seasons/Hours:	Year-round: 10 am–4 pm Tu–F; summer (May–Aug): 10 am–3 pm Sa; or by appointment
Cost:	Free, donations accepted
Address:	Hwy 2 W, Shevlin, MN 56676
Mailing Address:	Clearwater County Historical Society, PO Box 241, Bagley, MN 56621
Phone:	218.785.2000
E-mail:	cchshist@gvtel.com
Directions:	Located on Hwy 2 in Shevlin, seven mi. E of Bagley.

EAST POLK COUNTY HERITAGE CENTER

⑩ *Description:*	Explore the 100-year-old restored Larson House, in which the upstairs has been converted to a medical room, school room, press room, nursery and bathroom. The house is furnished with antiquities of its time, including a 100-year-old piano that once belonged to the Fosston Opera House. Also on site is a log cabin and a 1914 Ford touring car, as well as the cabin of Cordwood Pete, Paul Bunyan's 4-foot-9-inch kid brother.

Seasons/Hours:	Memorial Day–Labor Day 1:30 pm–4:30 pm Sa & Su or by appointment.
Cost:	Free
Address:	Hwy 2 E in Melland Park, PO Box 505, Fosston, MN 56542
Phone:	218.435.6136
Website:	www.fosston.com
Directions:	Off of Hwy 2 look for the museum sign on the north side.

ITASCA STATE PARK

⑪ *Description:*	As Minnesota's oldest state park, Itasca's rich history is reflected in the many things to do and see. Visit the Itasca Indian Cemetery, the WPA buildings, Wegmann's Cabin or the bison kill site dating back to 9,000 BC.
Seasons/Hours:	Daily: 9 am–7 pm
Cost:	State park permit: $12-$20; day-use sticker: $4; camping fees: $7-$14.50
Address:	36750 Main Park Dr, Park Rapids, MN 56470
Phone/Fax:	Ph: 218.266.2100 (General information summer); Fax: 218.266.3942
E-mail:	itasca.park@dnr.state.mn.us
Website:	www.dnr.state.mn.us/state_parks/itasca/index.html
Directions:	From Bemidji, take Hwy 71 S 30 mi. From Park Rapids, take Hwy 71 N 21 mi.

SAUM HISTORICAL LOG SCHOOL

⑫ *Description:*	In 1903 this log school was built in Saum, which later consolidated with schools in the nearby towns of Battle River and Foy. This is the first consolidated school after state legislature passed the School Consolidation Act of 1911. This National Historic Site includes Saum's original log school and all its original furnishings.
Seasons/Hours:	Open by appointment
Cost:	Free
Mailing Address:	Arnold Wolden, HS 79, Box S-41, Saum, MN 56674

Phone:	218.647.8877
Directions:	Saum is located near the Upper Red Lake west of Kelliher on Cty Rd 34.

BECKER COUNTY HISTORICAL SOCIETY AND MUSUEM

(13) *Description:*	Visitors will find extensive research and genealogical materials at the Becker County Historical Society and Museum. This museum is also home to exhibits ranging from natural history to pioneer life, including a reconstructed original log cabin, a full-sized wigwam and a replica of the world's smallest gas station.
Seasons/Hours:	Year-round: 9 am–5 pm, Tu–Sa
Cost:	Free
Address:	714 Summit Ave, PO Box 622, Detroit Lakes, MN 56501
Phone:	218.847.2938
E-mail:	bech39@beckercountyhistory.org
Website:	www.beckercountyhistory.org
Directions:	Go downtown Detroit Lakes just off of Hwy 10 to Summit St and W Front St.

FINN CREEK MUSEUM

(14) *Description:*	The nearby creek that meandered through the predominantly Finnish region was named Finn Creek. The Finnish family Tapio homesteaded this 1900 farm site resting near the creek. To preserve the Finnish heritage, this museum has restored the original farmhouse and sauna, and added a schoolhouse, a sawmill and a summer kitchen, to name a few.
Seasons/Hours:	Memorial Day–Labor Day: 1 pm–5 pm daily
Cost:	Free
Address:	55442 340th St, New York Mills, MN 56567
Phone:	218.385.2233
E-mail:	dmaedenprairiemn@aol.com
Website:	www.explorenewyorkmills.com/html/finn_creek.html
Directions:	Three mi. E of New York Mills on US Hwy 10, to Hwy 106, S 2½ mi., then ½ mi. W on gravel road, or 4½ mi. N of Deer Creek on Hwy 106. Museum signs are posted on Hwy 106.

HISTORY MUSEUM OF EAST OTTER TAIL COUNTY

⑮ *Description:* The History Museum of East Otter Tail County is located in a historic stone structure originally built in 1887 as an Episcopal Church. The museum's focus is on the buildings, people, work and play from the area.

Some samples of the displays include the following: the Schroeder's Brewery in Perham, Drahmann's Department Store that was started in 1876 in Rush Lake, Clark & McClure Logging Company in 1876, the forgotten towns of East Otter Tail County, a Native American collection, the Otter Tail River, the early days of medicine, pioneer quilts, the Perham Telephone Company and railroads of the area. Genealogical resources are on site, and online local historical records and photos are also available.

Seasons/Hours: Year-round: 10 am–5 pm M–Sa; 1 pm–4 pm Su

Cost: Free

Address: 230 1st Ave N, Perham, MN 56573

Phone: 218.346.7676

E-mail: museum@eot.com

Website: www.historymuseumEOT.org/

Directions: In Perham, go one block NE of the railroad between 2nd Ave NE and 2nd Ave NW.

OLD CROSSING AND TREATY PARK

⑯ *Description:* In the mid-1800s, this park is where ox cart trains crossed the Red Lake River. The Red Lake and Pembina bands of the Chippewa Indians signed a treaty in 1863 that ceded 11 million acres of land on both sides of the Red Lake River to the US Government. Alexander Ramsey represented the US as the treaty governor, citing the main object as securing "the uninterrupted navigation of the Red River of the North."

Today, this beautiful park offers primitive camping and excellent fishing.

Seasons/Hours: Year-round

Cost: Free

Write to: Red Lake County Historical Society, c/o Anne Healy, 135 Bottineau Ave NE, Red Lake Falls, MN 56750

Phone: 218.253.2833

Directions:	From Crookston, follow Cty Rd 11 E from Hwy 2 through Gentilly. Turn W on Cty Rd 3 and follow the river roads about two mi. to Old Crossing.

From Thief River Falls, go 16 mi. S on Hwy 32 to Red Lake Falls, then to Cty Rd 11 and turn W on Cty Rd 3 to the park. |

OLD HOMETOWN MUSEUM

⑰ *Description:*	Old Hometown Museum brings its visitors back to early Stephen with many artifacts, including an old-fashioned kitchen and antique furniture. The building is filled with items such as farm machinery—much of the pieces horse-drawn—and tools that early settlers used. The museum holds such activities as the Pie and Ice Cream Social or the Polish Sausage Luncheon. Come for some good food and socializing.
Seasons/Hours:	Sunday afternoons in the summer
Cost:	Free
Address:	608 5th St, Stephen, MN 56757
Phone:	218.478.2456
Directions:	Go two blocks W of the railroad at the intersection of Stephen Ave and 5th St.

OLD MILL STATE PARK

⑱ *Description:*	This park was first homesteaded by Lars Larson, a Swedish immigrant, in 1882. Park visitors can actually take in the sights, sounds and smells of a Case 359 steam-powered flour mill in operation. Once a year, usually the last Sunday in August, spectators are invited to witness the grist mill grind flour. There is also a log cabin on site, as well as interpretive signs along trails that wind through the park.
Seasons/Hours:	Year-round: 8 am–10 pm daily; office: 9 am–4 pm daily
Cost:	State park annual permit: $12–$25; daily permit: $7; camping fees: $7–$18 per night (2004)
Address:	33489 240th Ave NW, Argyle, MN 56713
Phone:	218.437.8174
Website:	www.dnr.state.mn.us/state_parks/old_mill
Directions:	11 mi. W of Newfolden on Cty Rd 4., or 13 mi. E of Argyle on Cty Rd 4. Access to the park is 1/2 mi. off Cty Rd 4.

PEDER ENGELSTAD PIONEER VILLAGE

(19) Description: Peder Engelstad Pioneer Village offers the public a unique opportunity to walk through a replica of a Northern Minnesota pioneer town with beautiful vintage gardens as it might have been 100 years ago. Pioneer Village houses many artifacts from the past displayed in 19 buildings, including two railroad depots, a one-room schoolhouse, a church, a general store and a Victorian house, to name a few. Many pieces of farm machinery are also on display and an extensive research collection of print materials is available for use.

Seasons/Hours: Memorial Day–Labor Day: 1 pm–5 pm daily, tours are available upon request

Cost: Adults: $3, children age 12 and under: free with an adult

Address: 825 Oakland Park Rd, PO Box 127, Thief River Falls, MN 56701

Phone: 218.681.5767

E-mail: pchstrf@mncable.net

Website: www.ci.thief-river-falls.mn.us/community/pioneer.htm

Directions: SE of Thief River Falls on Hwy 32 to Oakland Park Rd.

POLK COUNTY MUSEUM

(20) Description: Polk County Museum's main building has several rooms with displays on everything from musical instruments to early farm tools. Other rooms include a kitchen, bedroom, parlor, general store, dentist office, doctor's office, barber shop, beauty shop and a communication room. Look for the largest Red River ox cart on the museum lawn.

Seasons/Hours: Late May–mid-Sept 1 pm–5 pm daily, winter months open by appointment

Cost: Free

Address: 719 E Robert St, Crookston, MN 56716

Phone: 218.281.1038

Directions: From Crookston, go E on Hwy 2 to the edge of town.

12,000 years ago, Crookston and the surrounding area was covered with nearly 300 feet of water from the glacial Lake Agassiz, which went on to form the Red River.

SETTLERS' SQUARE

㉑ *Description:* Settlers' Square is a collection of original and replica buildings dating back to 1880s–1930s, including the Alma Lutheran Church, built in 1893, and the Soo Line Railroad Depot. Get a flavor of the area by checking out the collection of early farm machinery. See the one-of-a-kind cattail bailer, used to harvest cattails, which were then used for stuffing in WWII life preservers. Some other features include Minnesota's only "cook car" and the deputy sheriff's car that was mysteriously damaged by a UFO in 1979. School tours are welcome.

Seasons/Hours: May–Sept: 9 am–5 pm W–F; tours by request (call for exact dates)

Cost: Free, donations appreciated

Address: 808 E Johnson Ave, PO Box 103, Warren, MN 56762

Phone: 218.745.4803 or 218.478.2743

Directions: Warren is on Hwy 1 between East Grand Forks and Thief River Falls. Settlers' Square is on the eastern edge of Warren on the fairgrounds.

OTTER TAIL COUNTY HISTORICAL MUSEUM

㉒ *Description:* A visit to the Otter Tail Historical Museum starts with the heirloom garden. This is a public garden that uses vegetable, herb and flower seeds saved from season to season to preserve and grow rare varieties. Stroll through the garden and read interpretive signs describing the plants. The museum offers over 100 permanent and changing exhibits. There is a Natural History Discovery room for kids in a log cabin. A research library is available for public use, and a gift shop features many handcrafted gifts, Native American crafts, books and heirloom seeds.

Seasons/Hours: Daily exhibit gallery: 9 am–5 pm M–F;
1 pm–4 pm Sa; 1 pm–4 pm Su (June–Aug only);
research library: 9 am–5 pm M–F

Cost: Free

Address:	1110 W Lincoln, Fergus Falls, MN 56537
Phone/Fax:	Ph: 218.736.6038; Fax: 218.739.3075
E-mail:	otchs@prtel.com
Website:	www.fergusfalls.com/tourism/museum.html
Directions:	From Fergus Falls, go N on Hwy 59.

PHELPS MILL

㉓ *Description:* The Phelps Mill tells the story of milling in rural Minnesota. Otter Tail County was the largest flour-producing area west of Minneapolis. The Maine Roller Mills, as it was originally named, began grinding wheat in 1889. The success of the mill prompted a three-story addition to grind buckwheat and rye in 1895. But after a drought and with the uprising of the Twin Cities' electric and steam-powered mills with easy access to the railroad, this rural mill closed in 1939. Complete with original operating machinery still in place, it is now on the National Register of Historic Places.

Seasons/Hours:	Call ahead for hours
Cost:	Free
Address:	29035 Cty Hwy 75, Underwood, MN 56586
Phone/Fax:	Ph: 218.736.6038; Fax: 218.739.3075
E-mail:	Otchs@yahoo.com
Website:	www.co.otter-tail.mn.us/phelpsmill/
Directions:	From Underwood, go N on Main St (Hwy 35) to 230th Ave E. It will curve N and turn into 310th Ave to the mill.

 An 8,000-year-old woman was found near Pelican Rapids in 1932. Named "Minnesota Woman," experts believe that she drowned when she was 15.

CLAY COUNTY
HISTORICAL SOCIETY

㉔ *Description:* The Historical Society has changing and permanent exhibits, the latter featuring the different modes of transportation used by the people of an earlier era. The collection includes Red River carts, bicycles, steamboats and street cars.

Seasons/Hours:	Year-round: 10 am–5 pm M–Sa (10 am–9 pm Tu); 12 pm–5 pm Su
Cost:	Free
Address:	202 1st Ave N, Moorhead, MN 56560
Phone:	218.299.5520
E-mail:	lisa.hanson@ci.moorhead.mn.us
Website:	www.info.co.clay.mn.us/history
Directions:	From I-94 in Moorhead, take Exit 1 N (or go N on Hwy 75). Turn left onto 1st Ave N. Turn right after the 2nd stoplight.

COMSTOCK HOUSE

㉕ *Description:* The Comstock House was built in 1882. It contains the original furnishings including tapestries, china and crystal. Visitors taking the guided tour can hear stories about Solomon

Minnesota Historical Society

Comstock House

Comstock, a lawyer who moved to Moorhead in 1871. Comstock's contributions to his community include establishing the First National Bank and Moorhead State University. He also worked with James J. Hill to build a railroad system in the Red River Valley, and in 1889 he became a US Congressman.

Seasons/Hours:	Memorial Day–Sept (call for exact dates) 1 pm–4:15 pm Sa & Su; year-round by appointment
Cost:	Adults: $4, senior citizens: $3, children 6-12: $2; children under 6 and MNHS members: free
Address:	506 8th St S, Moorhead, MN 56560
Phone:	218.291.4211
E-mail:	comstock@mnhs.org
Website:	www.mnhs.org/places/sites/ch/index.html
Directions:	From I-94 W, take Exit 1A onto Hwy 75 S toward Moorhead. Turn right onto 8th St.

HERITAGE HJEMKOMST INTERPRETIVE CENTER

㉖ Description: The Heritage Hjemkomst Interpretive Center gives interpretation of the heritage of the Red River Valley. The Center offers educational exhibits, programs, tours, festivals, lectures and performances. It is home to the Hjemkomst Viking Ship and a replica of the Norwegian Hopperstad Stavkirke.

See the 76-foot-long Hjemkomst Viking Ship, along with a videotape chronicling the construction of the ship and its voyage across the Atlantic.

The Stavekirke, Norwegian for "stave church," was modeled after the Hopperstad church in Norway, which was restored in 1885 and is one of 29 remaining stavekirkes in Norway. The Moorhead Stavekirke was opened to the public in 1998.

Seasons/Hours: 9 am–5 pm M–Sa; 12 pm–5 pm Su

Cost: Adults: $6, senior citizens: $5, college students and children 5-17: $4, children 4 and under: free

Address: 202 1st Ave N, PO Box 157, Moorhead, MN 56561

Phone/Fax: Ph: 218.299.5511; Fax: 218.299.5510

E-mail: john.peterson@ci.moorhead.mn.us

Website: www.hjemkomst-center.com

Directions: From I-94 in Moorhead, take Exit 1 N (or go N on Hwy 75). Turn left onto 1st Ave N. Turn right after the 2nd stoplight.

NORMAN COUNTY HISTORICAL MUSEUM

㉗ Description: The Norman County Historical Society maintains several buildings with artifacts of past times. The Memorial Educational Museum and Prairie Village contain a variety of tools and machines used by early settlers.

Seasons/Hours: Year-round: 1 pm–5:30 pm Tu & Th

Cost: Free

Address: 104 1st Ave E, Ada, MN 56510

Phone: 218.784.4989 or 218.784.4141

E-mail: cgoltz@loretel.net

Website: www.rootsweb.com/~mnnorman/NCHistSoc.htm

Directions: From Hwy 9 in Ada, turn E on 1st Ave one block.

PRAIRIE VILLAGE

㉘ Description: Walk through a typical village that could be seen on the prairie landscape in the late 1800s. Step into the Pontoppidan Church which was built in 1891, and the Bethany Church, built in 1888. The bank contains original bank equipment and furniture. Other buildings include the country store, the depot from Luce, MN, the print shop and the Nordby Schoolhouse.

Seasons/Hours: May–Oct: 10 am–5 pm M; 9 am–5 pm Tu–F; 10 am–5 pm Sa; 1 pm–5 pm Su; or by appointment

Cost: Donation

Address: 12 1st St E, Ada, MN 56510

Phone: 218.784.4754

Directions: From Ada, go W on Hwy 200. Museum is on the south side.

STEVENS COUNTY HISTORY MUSEUM

㉙ Description: The Stevens County History Museum has exhibits and artifacts depicting pioneer life in Stevens County. Also see displays featuring local history and culture.

Seasons/Hours: Year-round: 9 am–5 pm M–F

Cost: Free, but charge for the library

Address: 116 W 6th St, Morris, MN 56267

Phone: 320.589.1719

E-mail: history@infolink.morris.mn.us

Directions: From Hwy 9 in Morris, go W 1½ blocks on 6th St.

TRAVERSE COUNTY HISTORICAL MUSEUM

㉚ Description: A one-room schoolhouse and a 1926 fire truck are some of sights to see at the Traverse County Historical Museum. Visitors will also find many intriguing items from the past and replicas of a meat market, a dentist office, home living quarters and a general store.

Seasons/Hours: Early May–Labor Day: 1 pm–5 pm W–Su

Cost: Free

Address:	Broadway W Hwy 27, Wheaton, MN 56296
Phone:	320.563.4110
E-mail:	sks@traversenet.com
Directions:	From Minneapolis, W on US 12 to N US 75 to W Hwy 27.
Don't miss this:	Take time to go two mi. W on Hwy 28/7 from Browns Valley to the wayside rest marking the Continental Divide. This is the point that water drains north to the Hudson Bay and the Minnesota River drains south to the Gulf of Mexico.
	About ½ mi. E of Browns Valley along Hwy 28/7 there is another wayside rest marking where the Browns Valley Man was found. In 1933 an archaeologist discovered a skeleton estimated to be 9,000 years old.

WILKIN COUNTY HISTORICAL SOCIETY

③1 *Description:*	Through donations this museum has grown from the basement of a bank to its current status of 8 antique-furnished rooms, including a living room, kitchen, hospital room, small chapel and bank. The museum also has farm machinery and many other smaller exhibits.
Seasons/Hours:	1:30 pm–4 pm Su, W & Th
Cost:	Free
Address:	704 Nebraska Ave, Breckenridge, MN 56520
Phone:	218.643.1303
Website:	www.mnhs.org/preserve/mho/chsclo.html
Directions:	In Breckenridge, go one block N of the railroad at the intersection of Nebraska Ave and 7th St N.

HUBBARD COUNTY HISTORICAL MUSEUM

③2 *Description:*	Striving to depict the history of the county, this museum has rooms with themes covering different aspects of the early life of the area. There is a heritage room, farming tools, logging items, clothing and war memorabilia. Step into a one-room school and a one-room pioneer home. Visit the North Country Museum of Arts which displays its collection of European paintings and revolving exhibits of contemporary artists.
Seasons/Hours:	May–Sept: 11 am–5 pm Tu–Su
Cost:	Free

Address:	301 Court Ave, Box 327, Park Rapids, MN 56470
Phone:	218.732.5237
Directions:	Go three blocks W of Hwy 71 on 3rd St.

RED RIVER MUSEUM

(33) *Description:*	Based on the book, "Red River: Paul Bunyan's Own Lumber Company and its Railroads," this friendly, family-run museum explores the history of lumber giant T.B. Walker. It can accommodate groups of 45 or more.
Seasons/Hours:	Memorial Day–Labor Day: by appointment M; 10 am–5 pm Tu–Sa; 12 pm–5 pm Su
Cost:	Adults: $4, children: $2, children 6 and under: free with a paid adult; groups of 10 adults or more: $3; schools with 10-25 students: $1.50 per child, drivers and teachers: free
Address:	Rt 1 Box 37, Akeley, MN 56433
Phone:	218.652.4371
Directions:	Go E three blocks from the intersection of Hwy 34 and Hwy 64.

HAYES LAKE STATE PARK

(34) *Description:*	Hayes Lake State Park contains the remains of an original homestead. The grave of homesteader Alva Hendershot can be seen along the trail just northwest of the dam. See the beautiful flowers and pick some blueberries too. Swim, canoe or just enjoy the outdoors.
Seasons/Hours:	Year-round: 9 am–4 pm daily
Cost:	State park permit: $12-$25; day-use sticker: $7; camping fees: $7-$20
Address:	48990 Cty Rd 4, Roseau, MN 56751-8745
Phone:	218.425.7504
Directions:	Entrance to the park is 15 mi. S of Roseau.

KITTSON COUNTY MUSEUM

35 Description: Specializing in turn-of-the-century history, this museum is home to many indoor and outdoor exhibits giving a taste of what life was like back then. The museum also holds records dating back as far as 1880. This site can accommodate large groups and is wheelchair accessible. Research and genealogy information is available.

Seasons/Hours: Year-round: 9 am–5 pm M–F; summer hours: 1 pm–5 pm Sa & Su

Cost: Free

Address: 332 E Main St, Lake Bronson, MN 56734

Phone: 218.754.4100

E-mail: history@wiktel.com

Website: www.nwrdc.org/kitt_info.htm

Directions: From Hwy 59 in Lake Bronson, go E on Main St 2½ blocks.

LAKE OF THE WOODS COUNTY HISTORICAL SOCIETY AND MUSEUM

36 Description: Visitors can check out exhibits on local and natural history, geology of the area, prehistoric human settlements, commercial fishing and logging. The Historical Society also maintains a re-creation of Fort St. Charles at the Northwest Angle, a fortress and trading post that was built in 1732 by Canadian-French voyageur Pierre LaVerendrye and his men. See the 1935 Norris CCC Camp, now the site of the Red Lake Wildlife Management Area Headquarters.

Seasons/Hours: May–Sept: 10 am–4 pm Tu–Sa

Cost: Free

Address: 119 8th Ave SE, PO Box 808, Baudette, MN 56623

Phone: 218.634.1200 or 218.634.2075

Directions: Take Hwy 73 to Hwy 11, turn left and go to 8th Ave SE.

PIONEER FARM AND VILLAGE

37 Description: There are many buildings of interest to explore at the Pioneer Farm and Village, including the Holm/Bjorkman building which houses a mural painted by Marv Espe, a local artist. Step inside the Nannestad Church and the Pinecreek Church. The log Pinecreek Lutheran Church is the oldest documented church in the county. Other areas to explore are the exhibit hall, pioneer museum, fellowship hall, trappers' cabin, lunch counter, post office, print shop and blacksmith shop.

Seasons/Hours:	May–Sept: 12 pm–5 pm M–F
Cost:	Free
Address:	Hwy 11 W, Roseau, MN 56751
Phone:	218.463.3052
Website:	www.stepintohistory.com/states/MN/Pioneer_village.htm
Directions:	From Roseau, go two mi. W on Hwy 11.

ROSEAU COUNTY HISTORICAL SOCIETY AND MUSEUM

(38) *Description:*	The Roseau County Historical Museum contains items from throughout the history of the county. Come and learn about Roseau or remember the area's past with pictures, videos, manuscripts and much more.
Seasons/Hours:	Winter: 9 am–4 pm Tu–F; summer: 9 am–5 pm Tu–F
Cost:	Free
Address:	110 2nd Ave NE, Roseau, MN 56751
Phone/Fax:	Ph: 218.463.1918; Fax: 218.463.3795
E-mail:	rchsroseau@mncable.net
Website:	www.roseaucohistoricalsociety.org
Directions:	From Hwy 11 in Roseau, go two blocks S on 2nd Ave NE.

Roseau is home to the Polaris Industries, builders of the first "iron dog" snow machine in 1954.

WARROAD PUBLIC LIBRARY AND HERITAGE CENTER

(39) *Description:*	This public library is also the center for historical information of early Warroad history. Come enjoy an enlightening afternoon of leisure reading or learning about the history of the Warroad area. Permanent exhibits explain the historical significance of commercial fishing on Lake of the Woods, mink ranching and

the Native Americans, to name a few.

Seasons/Hours:	1 pm–5 pm M–Sa; 1 pm–4 pm Su
Cost:	Free
Address:	202 Main St, Box H, Warroad, MN 56763
Phone/Fax:	Ph: 218.386.1283; Fax: 218.386.3408
Website:	www.nwrlib.org/warroad/heritage.htm
Directions:	From Minneapolis, N on I 35 to N MN 33, W US 2. Right on MN 46, left on US 71/MN 1, right on MN 1. Right on MN 72, go straight onto MN 11, right onto Lake St NE, left onto Main Ave NE to Warroad Road.
Don't miss this:	While in Warroad, get to the Old Canadian National Depot, listed on the National Register of Historic Buildings. 218.386.1454
	St. Mary's Catholic Church of Warroad is the largest log church in the state. The roof was constructed with 70,000 hand split cedar shakes. 218.386.1178

NORTHWEST MINNESOTA FESTIVALS

LISTED ALPHABETICALLY

 **ANNUAL GARDENER'S FESTIVAL AND NORTH CENTRAL REGIONAL FOLK FEST**

Description:	This fest has 7½ acres of gardens to tour, crafters, workshops, great food, activities for children and folk music on two different stages. The dollars raised go to local organizations.
Occurrence:	June
Write to:	7523 S 170th Ave, Sabin, MN 56580
Phone:	218.585.4252 or (701) 238.4303
E-mail:	onebigevent@aol.com
Directions:	20 min. S of the Fargo-Moorhead area. From Moorhead, take Hwy 52 S to Sabin. Turn S on 70th St and travel 11 mi. to 170th Ave E for ½ mi. Follow the signs for ONE BIG EVENT, or call for directions.

AWAKE THE LAKES

Description:	This is the Lakes area's kick-off to summer. Held at Alexandria's City Park and other locations throughout the city, it offers a wide range of activities throughout the weekend, including dinner in the park, a 5K run/walk, live entertainment, and antique car show. There are plenty of things for kids to do: the petting zoo, a pony ring, a kids' fishing contest, a carnival, fireworks and a street dance.
Occurrence:	Memorial Day weekend (F & Sa)
Write to:	206 Broadway, Alexandria, MN 56308
E-mail:	drydberg@alexandriamn.org
Phone:	320.763.3161 or 800.235.9441
Website:	www.alexandriamn.org
Directions:	Most events are at City Park, N of 3rd Ave on Nokomis St.

CHAUTAUQUA AND FESTIVAL OF HISTORY AND ARTS

Description:	This event features performers and music under the big tent. Clayworks demonstrations and workshops are performed by artists in a natural setting.
Occurrence:	Fourth weekend in August
Write to:	Red Lake County Historical Society, c/o Anne Healy, 135 Bottineau Ave, Red Lake Falls, MN 56750
Phone:	218.253.2833
E-mail:	annhealy@gvtel.com
Directions:	From Crookston, follow Cty Rd 11 E from Hwy 2 through Gentilly. Turn W on Cty Rd 3 and follow the river roads about two mi. to Old Crossing.
	From Thief River Falls, go 16 mi. S on Hwy 32 to Red Lake Falls, then to Cty Rd 11 and turn W on Cty Rd 3 to the Old Crossing and Treaty Park.

FLEKKEFEST

Description:	Flekkefest is an annual Scandinavian celebration filled with plenty of ethnic food, music, an all-town picnic, a parade and fireworks. Play in the softball tournament, join the eating contests, enter for the grand prize drawing or just take it all in and enjoy.
Occurrence:	First weekend in August
Write to:	Main St, Elbow Lake, MN 56531
Phone:	218.685.5380
E-mail:	chamber@runestone.net
Website:	www.flekkefest.com
Directions:	From Alexandria, take I-94 W 12 mi. to the Elbow Lake Exit. Then go 15 mi. W to Elbow Lake Main St.

GRAPE STOMP AND FALL FESTIVAL

Description:	This is the largest winery event of its kind. The Carlos Creek Winery Grape Stomp and Fall Festival features grape stomping that is sure to leave participants with stained feet and a lifetime of memories. There is live music and entertainment, over 150 craft booths and food booths to browse. There will be tours

throughout the event, an "I Love Lucy" look-alike contest, and a non-denominational church service in the vineyard on Sunday.

Occurrence:	September
Write to:	6693 Cty Rd 34 NW, Alexandria, MN 56308;
Phone/Fax:	Ph: 320.846.5443; Fax: 320.763.9290
E-mail:	ccwinery@carloscreekwinery.com
Website:	www.carloscreekwinery.com/grapestomp/
Directions:	From I-94 go N on Hwy 29 and turn right on 3rd Ave. Go one block to the next lights, then left on Cty Rd 42/Nokomis St. Turn left at Cty Rd 11/Cty Rd 34 fork, and follow Cty Rd 34. Carlos Creek Winery is two mi. N.

 ## MORRIS PIONEER DAYS

Description:	The whole family will enjoy a great weekend on the prairie in Morris. There are pony rides, a petting zoo, arts and crafts, musical performances, prairie wagon rides, a co-ed softball tournament, fireworks, a pancake breakfast and Grand Parade.
Occurrence:	Second weekend in July
Write to:	Morris Area Chamber of Commerce, 507 Atlantic Ave, Morris, MN 56267
Phone:	Chamber of Commerce Office: 320.589.1242
Website:	www.morrismnchamber.org/ppdays.html
Directions:	Most events take place at Eastside Park in Morris, located on 7th St just a few blocks E of Atlantic Ave (Hwy 9).

 ## OX CART DAYS FESTIVAL

Description:	Featuring music, a street fair, a 10k run, a kiddie parade, fireworks, a torchlight parade and a classic car show.
Occurrence:	August
Write to:	Crookston Chamber of Commerce, PO Box 115, 118 Fletcher St, Crookston, MN 56716-0115
Phone:	218.281.4320
E-mail:	crkchamber@rrv.net
Directions:	Central Park is located near downtown Crookston, just off of Robert St (Hwy 2 E).

PIONEER FARM FESTIVAL

Description:	This two-day festival at the Pioneer Farm and Village features events including demonstrations on the pioneer way of life, entertainment, a parade, children's games and events, threshing displays and antique tractors.
Occurrence:	August
Write to:	PO Box 307, 100 2nd Ave NE, Roseau, MN 56751
Phone:	218.463.1542 or 800.815.1824
E-mail:	tpetersn@wiktel.com
Directions:	From Roseau, go two mi. W on Hwy 11 to the Pioneer Farm and Village.

PIONEER FARMERS SHOW

Description:	A hot-air engine collectors' reunion, parades, logging and lumbering pageantry, music, threshing and engines on display at this event, held on the north side of Itasca State Park.
Occurrence:	Third weekend August (F–Su)
Write to:	Bob A. Bilden, Rt 3 Box 390, Bagley, MN 56621
Phone:	218.657.2233
Directions:	From Park Rapids, go 21 mi. N on Hwy 71, then 6 mi. NW on Hwy 200.

PIONEER FESTIVAL AND BLACK POWDER RENDEZVOUS

Description:	See how true pioneers lived, worked and played. Enjoy food, music and different demonstrations for a step back into the past.
Occurrence:	Third weekend in August
Write to:	135 E Main St, Perham, MN 56573
Phone/Fax:	Ph: 218.346.7710 or 800.634.6112; Fax: 218.346.7712 or 218.346.7676
E-mail:	museum@eot.com
Directions:	To the pioneer grounds, get to Hwy 10 exit to Perham, to the stoplight. Go to Hwy 80 (Main St.), take Cty Rd 8 E out of Perham by the stoplight to the edge of town, go about ten blocks. Look for pioneer village signs on the left.

RETURN TO THE PRAIRIE DAY

Description:	Experience the prairie by visiting the Prairie Wetlands Learning Center. Listen to music, stroll along trails through the prairie, and enjoy a variety of demonstrations on this Return to the Prairie Day.
Occurrence:	August
Write to:	602 Hwy 210 E, Fergus Falls, MN 56537
Phone/Fax:	Ph: 218.736.0938; Fax: 218.736.0941
E-mail:	prairiewet@fws.gov
Directions:	Take I-94 to Exit 57. Follow Hwy 210 E towards Fergus Falls. The entrance will be on the right about one mi.

RHUBARB FESTIVAL AND MIDSUMMER DAY CELEBRATION

Description:	Experience the heritage of Kittson County with this festival celebrating the popular "pie plant," rhubarb, and also the Swedish Midsummer Day.
Occurrence:	June
Write to:	PO Box 100, Lake Bronson, MN 56734
Phone:	218.754.4100
Directions:	From I-29, take US Hwy 81/Hwy 175 E to Hwy 59, then go S to Lake Bronson.

STEAM AND GAS SHOW AND THRESHING BEE

Description:	When you're in Roosevelt, you won't want to miss the parades, exhibits, demonstrations and great food. There is also a flea market, musicians, an old-time shingle mill, flour mill, thresher, working blacksmith shop and much more.
Occurrence:	Weekend of first Sunday in August
Phone/Fax:	Ph: 218.424.7395; Fax: 218.634.2915
E-mail:	lakwoods@wiktel.com
Directions:	From Warroad, go S on Hwy 5 to Hwy. 11 into Roosevelt. Then go N 9 mi. on Rocky Point Rd Event will be on left side.

 # SUMMERFEST

Description: Fergus Fall's summer festival has a huge arts and craft show and sale, kids' activities, food booths, a large parade and a street dance.

Occurrence: June

Phone: 218.736.6951

E-mail: chamber@prtel.com

Directions: From I-94, take Exit 54 to Lincoln Ave and go E to the stoplight by the gas station. Turn left and go two blocks to the Fergus Falls Community College, where most activities take place.

 ## SWEDISH LUCIA FEST

Description: A darkened banquet hall filled with 300 to 400 guests is silent while awaiting the presence of the chosen Lucia. As the music begins, the procession led by Lucia, begins to light the room. Soon the room is fully lighted by candles and the beautifully decorated banquet hall sparks the sense of the Christmas season's beginnings. This festive program includes music of high school and children's choirs, followed by a traditional Swedish breakfast.

Occurrence: December 13th, 6 am

Write to: Lloyd Johnson, 208 Norwood Dr NE, Bemidji, MN 56601

Phone: 218.444.3469

E-mail: lloydwj@webtv.net

Directions: From Bemidji, go W on Hwy 2 towards the airport. Banquet is at the Northern Inn, on the north side of the Hwy

 ## SWEDISH MIDSUMMER FESTIVAL

Description: One of Bemidji's annual celebrations, this special Swedish tradition welcomes the summer solstice with folk music and dancing on the beautiful downtown waterfront. A pole decorated with birch branches and fresh flowers is raised to symbolize the life and beauty of summer.

Occurrence: June

Write to:	Lloyd Johnson, 208 Norwood Dr NE, Bemidji, MN 56601
Phone:	218.444.3469
E-mail:	lloydwj@webtv.net
Directions:	In Bemidji, go to the intersection of Bemidji Ave and 3rd St.

 **TURTLEFEST**

Description:	Don't miss this awesome town festival. Many activities for the whole family: turtle races, a golf tournament, the area's largest quilt show, a street dance, kids' games, a demolition derby, a grand parade, fireworks, bed races and a lot more.
Occurrence:	June
Write to:	135 E Main St, Perham, MN 56573
Phone/Fax:	Ph: 218.346.7710 or 800.634.6112; Fax: 218.346.7712
E-mail:	chamber@perham.com
Website:	www.perham.com/turtlefest.asp
Directions:	70 mi. E of Fargo, ND on Hwy 10 or approximately three hours NW of Minneapolis.

 **WATERS OF THE DANCING SKY FESTIVAL**

Description:	This wide variety of activities includes birding field trips by land, water and horse-drawn wagon. Take in a riverboat cruise or one of many workshops on birds, mushrooms, wildflowers, painting, Native American heritage, wolves, owls, stargazing, Historic Fort St. Charles, canoeing, raptor rehab and more.
Occurrence:	Late May–early June
Write to:	Lake of the Woods Tourism, PO Box 518, Baudette, MN 56623
Phone/Fax:	Ph: 800.382.FISH (3474); Fax: 218.634.2915
E-mail:	lakwoods@wiktel.com
Directions:	Events are at various locations around Baudette.

 **WILD RICE DAYS**

Description:	Mahnomen is host to this festival which includes a parade, food stands, craft tables and a street dance.
Occurrence:	Third weekend in July
Phone:	218.935.2622
Website:	www.exploreminnesota.com/listing/index.cfm?id=6468
Directions:	From Detroit Lakes, go N on Hwy 59 to Mahnomen.

COUNTIES INCLUDED IN THIS SECTION:

BECKER COUNTY was established in 1858. It was named after Brigadier General George Loomis Becker who was one of three men elected to Congress in 1857. Since the state could only send two representatives, he stayed home with a promise made to him that the next county would be named for him. The county seat is Detroit Lakes. The area is 1,445 square miles, which ranges 14th in the state. Population is 30,000 people, which ranks 34th in Minnesota. Population density is 22.9 people per square mile, which ranks 49th in the state.

BELTRAMI COUNTY was established in 1866. It was named for Giacomo Constantino Beltrami, an Italian explorer who traveled through the area in 1823. The county seat is Bemidji. The area is 3,055 square miles, which ranks 4th in the state. Population is 39,650 people, which ranks 23rd in Minnesota. Population density is 15.8 people per square mile, which ranks 66th in the state.

CLAY COUNTY was established in 1858. It was named for Henry Clay who was a statesman and a one-time presidential candidate. The county seat is Moorhead. The area is 1,053 square miles, which ranks 20th in the state. The population is 51,229 people, which ranks 17th in Minnesota. Population density is 49 people per square mile, which ranks 27th in the state.

CLEARWATER COUNTY was established in 1902. It was named by the Ojibwe for its unusually clear lake and river. The county seat is Bagley. The area is 1,030 square miles, which ranks 21st in the state. Population is 8,423 people, which ranks 75th in Minnesota. Population density is 8.5 people per square mile, which ranks 78th in the state.

DOUGLAS COUNTY was established in 1866. It was named for Stephen Douglas, Illinois senator and presidential candidate who ran against Abraham Lincoln. The county seat is Alexandria. The area is 720 square miles, which ranks 41st in the state. Population is 32,821 people, which ranks 28th in Minnesota. Population density is 51.7 people per square mile, which ranks 26th in the state.

GRANT COUNTY was established in 1868. It was named for Ulysses S. Grant. The county seat is Elbow Lake. The area is 575 square miles, which ranks 61st in the state. Population is 6,289 people, which ranks 80th in Minnesota. Population density is 11.5 people per square mile, which ranks 72nd in the state.

HUBBARD COUNTY was established in 1883. It was named for Lucius Frederick Hubbard, who was governor of Minnesota from 1882 to 1887. The county seat is Park Rapids. The area is 999 square miles, which ranks 22th in the state. Population is 18,376 people, which ranks 50th in Minnesota. Population density is 19.9 people per square mile, which ranks 55th in the state.

KITTSON COUNTY was established in 1878. It was named for Norman W. Kittson, who was an early pioneer, trader, and politician. The county seat is Hallock. The area is 1,103 square miles, which is 19th in the state. Population is 5,285 people, which ranks 82nd in Minnesota. Population density is 4.8 people per square mile, which ranks 84th in the state.

LAKE OF THE WOODS COUNTY was established 1922. It was named after the Lake of the Woods. The county seat is Baudette. The area is 1,775 square miles, which ranks 12th in the state. The population is 4,522 people, which ranks 85th in Minnesota. Population density is 3.5 people per square mile, which ranks 87th in the state.

MAHNOMEN COUNTY was established in 1906. It was named for the Ojibwe word for "wild rice." The county seat is Mahnomen. The area is 583 square miles, which is 59th in the state. Population is 5,190 people, which ranks 83rd in Minnesota. Population density is 9.3

people per square mile, which ranks 77th in the state.

NORMAN COUNTY was established in 1881. It was named for its high Norwegian population. The county seat is Ada. The area is 877 square miles, which ranks 26th in the state. Population is 7,442 people, which ranks 77th in Minnesota. Population density is 8.5 people per square mile, which ranks 79th in the state.

OTTER TAIL COUNTY was established in 1858. It was named for Otter Tail Lake which has a sandbar resembling an otter's tail. The county seat is Fergus Falls. The area is 2,225 square miles, which ranks 8th in the state. Population is 57,159 people, which ranks 13th in Minnesota. Population density is 28.9 people per square mile, which ranks 41st in the state.

PENNINGTON COUNTY was established in 1910. It was named for Edmund Pennington who was a prominent railroad executive. The county seat is Thief River Falls. The area is 618 square miles, which ranks 53th in the state. Population is 13,584 people, which ranks 61st in Minnesota. Population density is 22 people per square mile, which ranks 52nd in the state.

POLK COUNTY was established in 1858. It was named for James K. Polk, the 11th US President. The county seat is Crookston. The area is 1,998 square miles, which ranks 9th in the state. Population is 31,369 people, which ranks 32nd in Minnesota. Population density is 15.9 people per square mile, which ranks 65th in the state.

RED LAKE COUNTY was established in 1896. It was named for the Red Lake River which flows through the county. The county seat is Red Lake Falls. The area is 432 square miles, which ranks 81st in the state. Population is 4,299 people, which ranks 86th in Minnesota. Population density is 10 people per square mile, which ranks 74th in the state.

ROSEAU COUNTY was established in 1894. It was named after the French word for "reeds," which grow in abundance in area lakes and rivers. The county seat is Roseau. The area is 1,678 square miles, which ranks 13th in the state. Population is 16,338 people, which ranks 54th in Minnesota. Population density is 9.8 people per square mile, which ranks 75th in the state.

STEVENS COUNTY was established in 1862. It was named for Isaac Ingalls Stevens who commanded the survey expedition for the Northern Pacific Railroad. The county seat is Morris. The area is 575 square miles, which ranks 60th in the state. Population is 10,053 people, which ranks 71st in Minnesota. Population density is 17.9 people per square mile, which ranks 59th in the state.

TRAVERSE COUNTY was established in 1862. It was named for Lake Traverse which is a French translation from the Dakota word meaning "lake lying crosswise." The county seat is Wheaton. The area is 586 square miles, which ranks 58th in the state. Population is 4,134 people, which ranks 87th in Minnesota. Population density is 7.2 people per square mile, which ranks 81st in the state.

WILKIN COUNTY was established in 1868. It was named for Colonel Alexander Wilkin who was a lawyer in St. Paul and served in the 9th Minnesota Regiment during the Civil War and later killed during battle in 1864. The county seat is Breckenridge. The area is 752 square miles, which ranks 35th in the state. Population is 7,138 people, which ranks 78th in Minnesota. Population density is 9.5 people per square mile, which ranks 76th in the state.

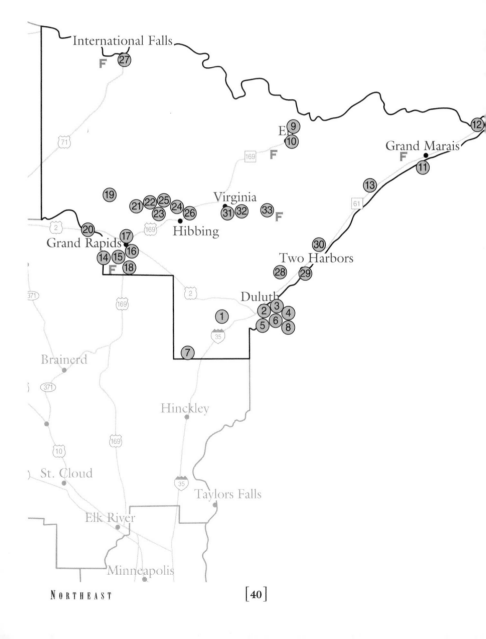

International Falls

F ㉗

E... ⑨
⑩

F

Grand Marais

F •

⑪

⑫

⑲

㉑ ㉒ ㉕
㉓ ㉔ ㉖

Virginia

㉛ ㉜

㉝ **F**

Hibbing

⑬

㉚

Grand Rapids

⑰
⑯
⑭ ⑮
F ⑱

Two Harbors

㉘ ㉙

Duluth

① ② ③ ④
⑤ ⑥ ⑧

⑦

Brainerd

Hinckley

St. Cloud

Taylors Falls

Elk River

Minneapolis

NORTHEAST MINNESOTA

ATTRACTIONS WITHIN AN HOUR'S DRIVE OF:

(#) = historic sites   F = festivals

CARLTON COUNTY HISTORY AND HERITAGE CENTER

① *Description:*	The Carlton County Heritage Center is housed in the old Cloquet Public library, which used the building until 1987. The Carlton County Historical Society operates the museum and maintains a reference library. The museum has information on the 1918 fire, which ravaged the area. There is also a model logging camp and other exhibits of pioneer artifacts.

Visitors can pick up a brochure for a self-guided tour through Cloquet. There are 21 sites listed on the tour. |
Seasons/Hours:	Year-round: 9 am–8 pm M; 9 am–4 pm Tu–F
Cost:	Free
Address:	Shaw Memorial Building, 406 Cloquet Ave, Cloquet, MN 55720
Phone:	218.879.1938
E-mail:	cchs@cpinternet.com
Website:	www.carltoncountyhs.org
Directions:	From I-35 N take the first Cloquet exit, take a right at the fourth stop light and go three blocks.

TRIVIA Cloquet is home to the only gas station designed by Frank Lloyd Wright.

FITGER'S BREWERY COMPLEX MUSEUM

② *Description:*	In 1859 the Fitger's beer ran so cold a stein had to be heated before the beer could be enjoyed. Within the bluestone walls of the renovated Fitger's Brewery, see the copper kettle and memorabilia from what was once one of the most successful breweries in the state. Enjoy a trip back in time to the brewing days, and see historic pictures and advertising throughout the museum. Spend a weekend at this complex, which offers shopping, dining, and Duluth's only AAA 4 Diamond Hotel.
Seasons/Hours:	Year-round: 10 am–5 pm M–F; 11 am–4 pm Sa; 12 pm–3 pm Su (seasonally open on weekends, call ahead)
Cost:	Free
Address:	600 E Superior St, Duluth, MN 55802

Phone:	218.722.8826 or 888.FITGERS (888.348.4377)
E-mail:	fitgers@fitgers.com
Website:	www.fitgers.com/history/
Directions:	Take I-35 to the Superior St. Exit. Go 13 blocks on Superior St. Fitger's is on the right.
Don't miss this:	Replica of a Viking Ship is in Leif Erikson Park. The park is at 10th Ave S and London Rd. There is a walking tour on which 24 homes can be seen on the east end of Duluth. A statue of the longest living Civil War veteran, Albert Woolson, is in Canal Park.

GLENSHEEN HISTORIC ESTATE

③ *Description:*	Completed in 1908 by Chester Congdon, Glensheen Historic Estate is on the National Register of Historic Places. The estate rests on seven acres along the shores of Lake Superior. The estate consists of the 39-room mansion, carriage house, gardener's cottage, clay tennis courts, beautiful gardens and more. The majority of the furnishings are original to the time the estate was first occupied. Costumed interpreters portray the servants and visitors to the house in the year 1915. A museum gift shop is also on site.
Seasons/Hours:	May 1–Oct 31; summer season: 9:30 am–4 pm daily Nov 1–Apr 30; winter season: 11 am–2 pm F–Su; Memorial Day–Labor Day: living history tours available by appointment
Cost:	General tours: adults: $9.50, seniors (62+) and juniors (12–15): $7.50, children (6–11): $4.50, children under 5: free; an additional hour-long tour of the third floor and attic is available: $10 per person
Address:	3300 London Rd., Duluth, MN 55804
Phone/Fax:	Ph: 218.726.8910 or 888.454.GLEN (888.454.4536); Fax: 218.726.8911
E-mail:	glen@d.umn.edu or info@glensheen.org
Website:	www.d.umn.edu/glen or www.glensheen.org
Directions:	N of Duluth on Hwy 61 past S 32nd Ave E.

LAKE SUPERIOR AND MISSISSIPPI RAILROAD

④ *Description:*	Take a 90-minute trip on a vintage train along the St. Louis River, lauded by the *St. Paul Pioneer Press* as the "Best Train Ride" in 2003. See the wildlife and beautiful scenery and expe-

rience life on an early railroad. As you ride the restored coaches, listen and learn about the history of what life was like in the days the railroad was the backbone of transportation of the growing nation.

Seasons/Hours: All weekends: June 12–Oct 3 (plus July 4 & Labor Day); departures at 10:30 am and 1:30 pm

Cost: Adults: $8, children under 12: $6

Address: Fremont St, PO Box 16211, Duluth, MN 55816

Phone/Fax: Ph: 218.627.7549; Fax: 218.728.6303

E-mail: info@lsmrr.org

Website: www.lsmrr.org

Directions: Take I-35 until the Cody St. Exit. Then go right on 63rd Ave W until Grand Ave. Take a right. Ticket office is at Fremont St and Grand Ave, opposite of Lake Superior Zoo.

LAKE SUPERIOR MARITIME VISITOR CENTER

⑤ *Description:* Check out a variety of exhibits, films and models and learn about the Twin Ports on Lake Superior and the ships that use them. Watch boats come through the canal under the Aerial Bridge. Call ahead—the museum will tailor a day of discovery depending on your schedule and educational desires.

Seasons/Hours: Call for exact dates. Winter (Oct–Mar): 10 am–4:30 pm F–Su; group tours on weekdays by appointment only; spring (Mar–May): 10 am–4:30 pm Su–Th, 10 am–6 pm F & Sa; summer (May–Oct): 10 am–9 pm daily

Cost: Free

Address: 600 Lake Ave S, Duluth, MN 55802

Phone/Fax: Ph: 218.727.2497; Fax: 218.720.5270

Directions: Take the 5th Ave W. Exit off of I-35. Turn left and go S on 5th Ave W.

There are five million acres of water in the state. Minnesota has more shoreline than Hawaii, California and Florida combined.

LAKE SUPERIOR RAILROAD MUSEUM

⑥ Description:
The Lake Superior Railroad Museum located in an 1892 depot that has one of the Midwest's largest collections of historic artifacts. Included is one of the world's largest locomotives, the oldest known rotary snowplow and a dining car china exhibit. Check out Depot Square where replicated storefronts represent Duluth in 1910. There is also a children's museum at the depot.

While at the depot during the months May to October, visitors can ride a train along the North Shore of Lake Superior. There are several options for trips, and reservations are suggested. Call for more information.

Seasons/Hours:
Memorial Day–mid-Oct: 9:30 am–6 pm daily;
Mid-Oct–Memorial Day: 10 am–5 pm M–Sa;
1 pm–5 pm Su

Cost: Adults: $8, children: $4.50

Address: 506 W Michigan St, Duluth, MN 55802

Phone:
Ph: 218.733.7590 or 800.423.1273;
for programs and tours, call 218.733.7594;
Fax: 218.733.7596

E-mail: museum@lsrm.org

Website: www.lsrm.org

Directions: Located in downtown Duluth. Exit off I-35 to W Michigan St down to the 5th Ave intersection.

MOOSE LAKE DEPOT AND FIRES OF 1918 MUSEUM

⑦ Description:
This old Soo Line Depot is on the National Register of Historic Places. The museum has exhibits on the area and the local railroads. The main emphasis is on the 1918 fires, which ended up destroying 250,000 acres, as well as taking the lives of 450 Moose Lake citizens. Come to the Depot to find out more about the tragedy of 1918.

Seasons/Hours:
May–Sept: 10 am–4 pm M, W–Sa; 12 pm–5 pm Su; other times by appointment

Cost: Free, donations appreciated

Address: 900 Folz Blvd, PO Box 235, Moose Lake, MN 55767

Phone: 218.485.4032 or 800.635.3680

E-mail: mlchamber@mooselake-mn.com

Website:	www.mooselake-mn.com/Pages/depot.html
Directions:	From Hwy 73, go 3½ blocks W of the downtown stoplights at the intersection of Hwy 27, on the left just off the Munger Bike Trail.
Don't miss this:	At the northern edge of Moose Lake, a 27-foot tall monument stands for the 453 who perished in the fire.

S.S. WILLIAM A. IRVIN

⑧ *Description:*	The *Irvin* was the first freighter built on the Great Lakes after the Depression in 1938, at a time when freighter design was highly conservative. Yet the *Irvin*, measuring longer than two football fields, incorporated many new technologies and lofty amenities such as a dining room, staterooms, shuffleboard and a driving range for golfers. It is the most visited ship on the Great Lakes.
	In October this floating museum gets into the spirit of Halloween and transforms into a haunted ship, complete with professional actors and equipment for special effects. Call for more information on tours.
Seasons/Hours:	Guided tours available May–Oct: 10 am–6 pm M–Th; 10 am–8 pm F & Sa
Cost:	Adults: $5.75, students: $4.25
Address:	301 Harbor Dr, Duluth, MN 55802
Phone/Fax:	Ph: 218.722.7876; Fax: 218.722.9206
E-mail:	omni@decc.org
Website:	www.williamairvin.com
Directions:	Take Exit 256B from I-35.

TRIVIA Lake Superior is the largest body of fresh water in the world. The maximum depth of the lake is 1,026 feet.

DOROTHY MOLTER MUSEUM

⑨ *Description:*	Dorothy Molter—known as the Root Beer Lady for her home-made root beer she offered to thirsty canoeists—lived in the Boundary Waters Canoe Area Wilderness (BWCAW) for 56 years. She was the last person to live within the BWCAW after

being granted lifetime tenancy. Stop by and enjoy a cold root beer as you walk through two of her cabins, filled with all her personal possessions.

Seasons/Hours:	Memorial Day–Labor Day: 10 am–5:30 pm M–Sa 12 pm–5:30 pm Su; daily in Sept; weekends in May
Cost:	Adults: $4, children 6–12: $2, children under 6: free
Address:	2002 E Sheridan, PO Box 391, Ely, MN 55731
Phone:	218.365.4451
E-mail:	dorothy@canoecountry.com
Website:	www.canoecountry.com/dorothy
Directions:	From Ely, head E on Hwy 169.

VERMILION INTERPRETIVE AND HISTORY MUSEUM

⑩ *Description:* The Vermilion Interpretive and History Museum has exhibits and artifacts from the Ely area. There is information about the area from the time of the voyageurs, through the development of iron ore mining to the present. The museum also has displays on the Will Steger and Paul Schurke Arctic Expedition.

Seasons/Hours:	Memorial Day–Labor Day: 10 a.m–5 pm daily
Cost:	Adults: $3, youth ages 5–15: $1
Address:	Vermilion Community College Complex, 1900 E Camp St, Ely, MN 55731
Phone:	218.365.3226
Directions:	20 mi. E of Tower Sudan on Hwy 16

Ely is home to the world-renowned International Wolf Center. Minnesota's timberwolf population is the second largest in the US only to Alaska.

COOK COUNTY HISTORICAL SOCIETY

⑪ *Description:* The Cook County Historical Society is located in an old light-house keeper's quarters that is listed on the National Register of Historic Places. Come experience the spirit of the land and learn about the Ojibwe Indians that lived on this land. The museum has artifacts, photos, and letters from the history of the county's people: the trappers, fishermen, miners and loggers that came from all over the world.

Seasons/Hours:	May–Oct: 10:30 am–4 pm Tu–Sa; 1 pm–4 pm M & Su
Cost:	Free
Address:	8 S Broadway, PO Box 1293, Grand Marais, MN 55604
Phone:	218.387.2883
Directions:	Go to Broadway in downtown Grand Marais.

GRAND PORTAGE NATIONAL MONUMENT

⑫ *Description:* Grand Portage National Monument is located in the Grand Portage Indian Reservation along Lake Superior. This reconstructed 1778 fort was the inland headquarters of the North West Fur Company. There is a kitchen, a great hall and the canoe warehouse. Examples of birch bark canoes essential to the fur trade are on display. Find the trailhead of the 8½-mile "Grand Portage," traveling around the rapids of the lower Pigeon River to Fort Charlotte and beyond to the interior waters, on which each voyageur carried two 90-pound "bales" across the trail.

Seasons/Hours:	Mid-May–mid-Oct: 9 am–5 pm daily
Cost:	Per person: $3, family: $6; with national park pass: free
Address:	Grand Portage National Monument (Headquarters), 315 S Broadway, PO Box 668, 211 Mile Creek Road, Grand Portage, MN 55605
Phone:	218.387.2788
E-mail:	pam_neil@nps.gov
Website:	www.nps.gov/grpo
Directions:	From Grand Marais, go 36 mi. N on Hwy 61, then 1 mi. E on Stevens Road. Watch for signs.

NORTH SHORE COMMERCIAL FISHING MUSEUM

⑬ *Description:* European immigrants began to settle along the North Shore of Lake Superior around 1890. The museum is dedicated to preserving their heritage and to telling the story of the early commercial fishing; this industry—a once-thriving contribution very significant to the livelihood of the settlers almost disappeared by the 1950s. There is a variety of exhibits, from the tools of the fishing industry to photos of the historic fish houses. Also hear stories of survival or the technique used to build a boat from the Fishermen's Voices Exhibit.

Seasons/Hours:	Summer: 9 am–7 pm daily; winter: 9 am–5 pm daily
Cost:	Adults: $3, children 12 and under: $1
Address:	7136 Hwy 61, PO Box 2312, Tofte, MN 55615
Phone:	218.663.7804
E-mail:	nscfm@boreal.org
Website:	www.commercialfishingmuseum.org
Directions:	On the lake side of Hwy 61 at the intersection of Hwy 61 and the Sawbill Trail (Cty Rd 2).

CHILDREN'S DISCOVERY MUSEUM

⑭ *Description:* This is a hands-on museum where children can enjoy the arts studio and music room, discover dinosaurs at the "Dino Dig," and meet "Treesa" the talking tree, among many others. A wide variety of permanent and changing educational exhibits are on display, as well as artifacts from *The Wizard of Oz*. Let children learn while they play through hands-on experiences.

Seasons/Hours:	Year-round: 10 am–5 pm daily
Cost:	Age 2 and older: $5 (includes admission to the Garland Birthplace)
Address:	2727 Hwy 169 S, PO Box 724, Grand Rapids, MN 55744
Phone:	Ph: 218.326.1900 or 800.CDM.KIDS (800.236.5437)
E-mail:	office@cdmkids.org
Website:	www.cdmkids.org
Directions:	Children's Discovery Museum is across from Home Depot on Hwy 169 S, two mi. from Hwy 2 in Grand Rapids.

FOREST HISTORY CENTER

⑮ *Description:* Lumberjacks cut more white pine trees in Minnesota during the winter of 1900 than ever before or ever since. Immerse yourself in this rich and romantic history by touring a re-created 1900 winter logging camp, listening as the camp workers tell their stories and experiencing the sights, sounds and smells of a bygone era. For the adventuresome, climb the 100-foot fire tower and hike the river, swamp and Forest of Today trails. Tour the visitor center exhibits and learn about past and contemporary forests and how they relate to our lives. Check the website for special programs and events.

Seasons/Hours:	June 1–Labor Day: 10 am–5 pm M–Sa; 12 pm–5 pm Su; school field trips and tour groups: May–Oct 15; call ahead for off-season and special tour hours and group rates; cross country ski and snowshoe trails open daily depending on conditions
Cost:	Adults: $6, senior citizens: $5, children ages 6–12: $4; children under 6 and MHS members: free
Address:	2609 Cty Rd 76, Grand Rapids, MN 55744
Phone:	218.327.4482
E-mail:	foresthistory@mnhs.org
Website:	www.mnhs.org/places/sites/fhc/
Directions:	From Grand Rapids, go S on Hwy 169, take a right onto Golf Course Rd., then another right onto Cty Hwy 76.

Minnesota Historical Society

Forest History Center

GARLAND BIRTHPLACE

⑯ *Description:* Judy Garland spent years of her childhood at this 1892 home. Restored to a 1925 time frame, the house is adjacent to a one-acre theme garden that is reminiscent of the classic movie, *The Wizard of Oz*, complete with a field of red poppies. Visit the gallery with Abe Lincoln's carriage from *The Wizard of Oz*,

Professor Marvel's Store and sit in on performances and documentary screenings.

Seasons/Hours:	Year-round: 10 am–5 pm daily
Cost:	Age 2 and older: $5 (includes admission to Children's Discovery Museum)
Address:	2727 Hwy 169 S, PO Box 724, Grand Rapids, MN 55744
Phone:	218.327.9276 or 800.664.JUDY (800.664.5839)
E-mail:	jgarland@uslink.net
Website:	www.judygarlandmuseum.com
Directions:	Judy's house is across from Home Depot on Hwy 169 S, two mi. S from Hwy 2 in Grand Rapids.

Judy Garland was born "Baby" Frances Ethel Gumm.

HISTORIC COLERAINE

⑰ *Description:* Located just north of Hibbing is the town of Coleraine. Stop at the Public Library or the City Hall to pick up a brochure for a self-guided tour through the streets of richly historic Coleraine. There are 14 sites; five of which are on the National Register of Historic Places. The sites include Greenway High School, Coleraine Village Hall, Company Housing District, the Kean Home, General Mining Superintendent's Home, Oliver Iron Mining Office, Coleraine Public Library, Longyear Park, Methodist Episcopal Church, Log Church, the Van Dyke Home, a Sears, Roebuck & Co. home, the Claypool Log Home and the Coleraine Ski Jump Site.

Directions: From Duluth, W on US 2 to N US 169. Right on Gayley Ave to Coleraine.

ITASCA HERITAGE CENTER

⑱ *Description:* The Heritage Center displays exhibits depicting the importance of the Native Americans, the lumber and iron ore industries and the Mississippi River at the turn of the twentieth century. There is information on the immigrants that came to the region and the simple home life that the early residents lived in the county.

The Heritage Center is also home to the Judy Garland Exhibit, a museum and a gift shop. Learn about the starlet's childhood and family, as she was born "Baby" Frances Ethel Gumm in Grand Rapids. The gift shop contains many unique ethnic and educational items, regional heritage books, and a great selection of *The Wizard of Oz* and Judy Garland gifts.

Seasons/Hours:	9:30–5 pm M–F; 10 am–4 pm Sa; 10 am–3 pm Su (summer only)
Cost:	Adults: $4, seniors: $3, children: $2
Address:	Old Central School, PO Box 66, 10 5th St NW, Grand Rapids, MN 55744
Phone:	218.326.6431
E-mail:	ichso@northernnet.com
Website:	www.visitgrandrapids.com/group_tours/attractions_02.html
Directions:	The Central School is at the intersection of Hwy 169 and Hwy 2 in downtown Grand Rapids.

JOYCE ESTATE

(19) *Description:* Chicago millionaire David Joyce, heir to a fortune that was made in part from lumber taken from the area, built this estate. The construction of the Adironack-style architecture around the beautiful, clear waters of Trout Lake was completed in 1935. The family continued to use the 4,500-acre estate until 1972. There are five areas to explore: the main lodge complex, the cabins on the hill, the garden greenhouse, the caretaker area, and the recreation area.

Take the 3½-mile trail to the Joyce Estate, or get there by boat via Trout Lake. A picnic site for day hikers and camping is available on the site of this millionaire's woodsy hideaway.

Seasons/Hours:	Year-round: daily
Cost:	Free
Address:	Marcell Office 49554, Hwy 38, Marcell, MN 56657
Phone:	218.832.3161
Website:	www.visitgrandrapids.com/vacations/recreation/forest_park.html
Directions:	Located 13 mi. N of Grand Rapids, one mi. E of the intersection of Cty Rd 60 and Hwy 38.

WHITE OAK FUR POST

Description: Buildings on this 40-acre reconstructed 1798 North West Company fur and trading post include the winter quarters for the voyageurs, a smokehouse, quarters for the clerks, a bourgeois and company store. Take a hike on the one-mile nature trail or camp in one of 26 private, wooded, primitive camping sites. Showers and kitchen facilities are available. Call to make arrangements.

A new Great Hall and Learning Center has been added to accommodate for up to 250 students grades K–12 during "School Days" held during the fur post's annual rendezvous. Students can relive the fur trade history in groups of 15 or less, and have a choice of 18 different small-group workshops. The Great Hall can also be rented on a half-day or weekend basis for families, groups, clubs or retreats, as well as colonial dinners or luncheons. Call for arrangements on special occasions.

Seasons/Hours: Annual rendezvous and public camping: the 1st full weekend in Aug; School Days: 1st week in May, call for dates in Oct; Tu–F 9:30 am–3:30 pm 10 am–7 pm Sa, 10 am–4 pm Su (times are flexible to serve individual needs)

Cost: Rendezvous: $6; School Days: students: $10; adults, teachers and chaperones: free; camping: $10 per night

Address: 33155 Hwy 6, Deer River, MN 56636

Phone/Fax: Contact Mary Jean Ph: 218.246.9393 leave message; Fax: 218.246.9393

E-mail: whiteoak@PaulBunyan.net or mjogee@email.com

Website: www.whiteoak.org

Directions: Take Hwy 2 W of Grand Rapids and go N on Hwy 6.

GREYHOUND BUS ORIGIN CENTER

Description: Hibbing is known as the Birthplace of the Bus Industry in the US. The Greyhound Bus Museum tells this story of how, with a 1914 Hupmobile they could not sell and a two-mile route, Greyhound was born. The visitor passes through a tunnel with motor sounds of 1914. Then with pictorial displays, audiovisual presentations, a movie, historical buses and hundreds of artifacts and memorabilia, the story is told from the past to present.

Seasons/Hours: Mid-May–late Sept: 9 am–5 pm M–Sa; 1 pm–5 pm Su

Cost: Adults: $3; students: $2; children 6–12: $1

Address:	1201 Greyhound Blvd, Hibbing, MN 55746
Phone:	218.263.5814
E-mail:	gom@cpinternet.com
Website:	www.irontrail.org/Attractions/museums/Greyhound+Bus+Museum
Directions:	From Howard St, turn N on 3rd Ave, go across the railroad tracks and look for the large gray building.

HIBBING HISTORICAL MUSEUM

㉒ *Description:* The museum has many pictorial displays and artifacts from the history of the area. There are exhibits of logging and mining with pictures showing how the tools were used. There is a model of Hibbing of how it looked in 1893, as well as a model of how the town looked in 1913 when it was forced to move. Audio-visual presentations explain the history of the area. The town of Hibbing was named for Frank Hibbing. He discovered iron ore on the Mesaba Range and in 1893 platted the town of Hibbing.

Seasons/Hours: May–Sept: 9 am–4 pm M–Sa; Sept–May: 10 am–3 pm M–F; other times by appointment

Cost: Adults $4, children 12 and under free

Address: Memorial Building, 400 23rd St, Hibbing, MN 55746

Phone: 218.263.8522

E-mail: hibbhist@uslink.net

Website: www.irontrail.org/attractions/museums/Hibbing+Historical+Museum

Directions: From Hwy 169, go N on 23rd St. Go seven blocks (½ mi.) to the Hibbing Memorial Building on your left. The museum is in the basement.

HULL RUST MAHONING MINE

㉓ *Description:* This National Historic Landmark is the world's largest iron ore pit, stretching 2 miles wide, 3 miles long and 535 feet deep. It was the first strip mine and open pit mine on the Mesabi Iron Range. There is a park with picnic facilities, trucks to play on and an observation area in north Hibbing.

Seasons/Hours: Jun 1–Aug 31: 9 am–6 pm; Sept 1–late Sept: 9 am–5 pm; tours by appointment

Cost: Free

Address:	Hull Rust Mahoning Mine, 401 Penobscot Rd., Hibbing, MN 55746
Phone:	218.262.4166
E-mail:	info@irontrail.org
Directions:	From Hwy 169 take Howard St nine blocks to 3rd Ave E. Go right, pass the Greyhound Museum and follow the signs.

IRON ORE MINER MEMORIAL

㉔ *Description:*	This statue is located on the west side of Chisholm at the entrance to Hwy 169. The memorial stands 87 feet high and weighs 150 tons. It stands in honor of the miners who worked to provide iron ore that helped win two World Wars and build up the United States. It is the nation's third largest free-standing statue.
Seasons/Hours:	Year-round
Cost:	Free
Write to:	Chisholm Chamber of Commerce, 10 NW 2nd Ave, Chisholm, MN 55719
Phone:	800.372.6437
Directions:	Located at the west entrance to Chisholm on Hwy 169.

IRONWORLD DISCOVERY CENTER

㉕ *Description:*	Experience the story of the Iron Range mining and immigration: the life, the work, the place and the people. Ironworld offers a museum and library, outdoor exhibits, education programs and a 2½-mile trolley excursion along an open pit mine to an old mining location.
Seasons/Hours:	Museum and trolley open seasonally. Research library and archives open year-round: call for hours.
Cost:	Adults: $8, seniors (62+): $7, youth ages 7–17: $6, children under 6: free; families: $24
Address:	801 SW Hwy 169, Suite 1, Chisholm, MN 55719
Phone:	218.254.7959 or 800.372.6437
E-mail:	marketing@ironworld.com
Website:	www.ironworld.com
Directions:	On Hwy 169 in Chisholm, go E of the Hwy 73 intersection.

MINNESOTA MUSEUM OF MINING

 Description: Tour buildings with displays of mining life. See examples of town life, shops, mining trucks and a 1910 steam locomotive. There is a simulated underground shaft. While you are there, watch a slide show or go on a self-guided tour through the museum.

Seasons/Hours: Summer: 9 am–5 pm M–Sa; 1 pm–5 pm Su

Cost: Adults: $3, students: $2, children 5 and under: free

Address: 701 Lake St W, PO Box 271, Chisholm, MN 55719

Phone: 218.254.5543

Directions: Go towards the water tower on Main St in downtown Chisholm.

KOOCHICHING MUSEUMS

 Description: Koochiching County Historical Museum has a collection of artifacts pertaining to the history of the county. There are exhibits featuring historical documentary on the region's Native Americans and culture, European settlement, fur trade and forestry.

Raised in International Falls, Bronko Nagurski may have been the greatest football player of all time. After his death in 1990, a museum dedicated to him was added onto the Koochiching County Historical Society. The museum has exhibits about Bronko Nagurski and the influential role he played in the evolution of the sport of football. Bronko memorabilia is available for purchase.

Seasons/Hours: Year-round: 9 am–5 pm M–F

Cost: Adults: $2, students: $1; preschoolers and members of Koochiching County Historical Society: free

Address: 214 6th Ave, International Falls, MN 56649

Phone: 218.283.4316

Directions: In International Falls, head N off of Hwy 71 on 6th Ave.

 The county seat, International Falls, is known as the nation's icebox.

3M DWAN MUSEUM

㉘ Description: This is the original restored office building that became the birthplace of 3M. Exhibits include a history of the company, a re-creation of attorney John Dwan's office, photos, artifacts, a lab and hands-on interactive programs. This building is now listed on the National Register of Historic Places.

Seasons/Hours: May–Oct: 12:30 pm–5 pm M–F; 9 am–5 pm Sa; 10 am–3 pm Su; other times by appointment

Cost: Adults: $2.50, youth 9-17: $1, children 8 and under free

Address: 201 Waterfront Dr, Two Harbors, MN 55616

Phone: 218.834.4898

E-mail: lakehist@lakenet.com

Directions: Located on Waterfront Dr, five blocks S of Hwy 61.

3M™ started in Two Harbors in 1902 but was not successful until 1916 when they released their first exclusive product, the Three-M-ite™ Abrasives Cloth.

LAKE COUNTY HISTORICAL MUSEUM

㉙ Description: The 1907 headquarters of the Duluth & Iron Range Railroad is the home of the Depot Museum. In 1884 the first load of iron ore was shipped from Two Harbors. An exhibit in this museum tells the story through words and pictures of this first shipment. Separate rooms in the museum are dedicated to depicting the life of children during pioneer days, of veterans, and of the famous dog-sledding mailman, John Beargrease.

Seasons/Hours: 9 am–5 pm M–Sa; 10 am–3 pm Su

Cost: Adults: $2, children 9-17: $1, 8 and under: free

Address: 520 S Ave, Two Harbors, MN 55616

Phone: 218.834.4898

Website: www.northshorehistory.com/sites/depot.html

Directions: Go S of Hwy 61 to South Ave between 5th and 6th St.

SPLIT ROCK LIGHTHOUSE

㉚ Description: Split Rock Lighthouse was built in 1909 after the disastrous storms of 1905. The lighthouse keeper's house, the fog-signal building and the lighthouse have been restored to their 1920s state. There is a history center containing many exhibits and a film about the building of the lighthouse and the lives of the early lighthouse keepers. Costumed characters and tour guides will lead the way through the lighthouse. Stop by the museum store for lighthouse memorabilia to take home.

Seasons/Hours: May 15–Oct 15: 10 am–6 pm daily

Cost: Adults: $8, senior citizens: $7, children 6-12: $6; children under 6 and MHS members: free

Address: 3713 Split Rock Lighthouse Rd., Two Harbors, MN 55616

Phone: 218.226.6372 or 888.PAST.FUN

E-mail: splitrock@mnhs.org

Website: www.mnhs.org/place/sites/srl/

Directions: Located in Split Rock Lighthouse State Park, 20 mi. NE of Two Harbors on Hwy 61.

Minnesota Historical Society

Split Rock Lighthouse

(31) Description: The Heritage Museum's main building contains artifacts, photographs and displays from the history of the area. Learn about the Virginia and Rainy Lake Sawmill Company which was the biggest white pine sawmill company in the world at one time, the two fires that decimated the town of Virginia and the trolley line that crossed the Iron Range. See a furnished 1910 log house built by a Finnish immigrant, Oscar Holkko. The third building is a tourist cabin built by the city to promote tourism in the '30s, housing exhibits on beauty and barber shops and dentistry. Changing exhibits are found throughout the complex The museum welcomes tour groups and classes, and the public to use the archives for research. Buildings are handicapped accessible.

Seasons/Hours: Oct–April: 11 am–4 pm Th–Sa;
May–Sept: 11 am–4 pm Tu–Sa

Cost: $1 donation; children are free

Address: 800 9th Ave N, Virginia, MN 55792

Phone: 218.741.1136

E-mail: virghist@virginiamn.com

Website: www.irontrail.org/attractions/museums/virginia+area+historical+society+museum/

Directions: In Virginia, exit off Hwy 53 onto 9th St. At 9th St and 9th Ave, take a right. Go one block and the museum is on your right.

Don't miss this: While visiting the Olcott Park check out some examples of from the Civilian Works Administration and the Works Project Administration. These projects include the planting of over 1000 trees and a three-acre rock garden. In 1937 General Electric Company completed an illuminated fountain.

IRON RANGE HISTORICAL SOCIETY

(32) Description: The society maintains photographs, weekly newspapers from the area, family histories and Iron Range memorabilia. There is also a large collection of law enforcement artifacts. Information on Will Steger, a famous explorer, and his North Pole Expedition can also be found in the museum.

Seasons/Hours: Year-round: 9 am–2 pm M & Tu; call ahead for special winter hours

Cost:	Memberships: annual $10; club $20/year; business $35/year; life $100/year
Address:	19 S Broadway St, PO Box 786, Gilbert, MN 55741
Phone:	218.749.3150
Website:	www.irontrail.org/attractions/museums/iron+range+historical+society+museum/
Directions:	Located on S Broadway St (Hwy 37) in Gilbert.

LONGYEAR DRILL SITE

㉝ *Description:*	It is registered as both a state and a national historic site. This site is where Edmund Longyear took charge of the first Iron Range drilling operation. There is a parking area with information directing visitors along a nature trail to the exploratory drill site.
Seasons/Hours:	Year-round, daily
Cost:	Free
Address:	Cty Rd 666, Hoyt Lakes, MN 55750
Phone:	218.749.3150
E-mail:	info@irontrail.org
Website:	www.irontrail.org/attractions/mining/longyear+drill+site
Directions:	From St. Louis Cty Rd 110, go N on Cty Rd 666 about 3½ mi.

NORTHEAST MINNESOTA FESTIVALS

LISTED ALPHABETICALLY

 **FISHERMAN'S PICNIC**

Description:	Tournaments are held for fishing, tennis, basketball and softball enthusiasts. This event has games, music, a fish burger stand, vendors, a Crazy Daze Sale and much more. Come spend the day in Grand Marais.
Occurrence:	First weekend in August
Write to:	Fisherman's Picnic, PO Box 176, Grand Marais, MN 55604
Phone/Fax:	218.387.2524
Directions:	Follow Hwy 61 N to Grand Marais.

 **HOYT LAKES WATER CARNIVAL**

Description:	A three-day carnival featuring waterski shows, open air dances, turtle races, in-line skating race, 5K race, fireworks, pancake feed and parade, softball, volleyball and tennis tournaments.
Occurrence:	Fourth weekend in July
Cost:	Admission: $5; children 12 and under: free
Write to:	PO Box 219, Hoyt Lakes, MN 55750
Phone/Fax:	Ph and Fax: 218.225.2617
E-mail:	info@hoytlakescarnival.com
Website:	www.hoytlakescarnival.com/
Directions:	From the Twin Cities, go N on I-35 to Exit 237 towards Cloquet. Turn N (left) onto US Hwy 53 to Gilbert, then W (right) on MN Hwy 37 and N on Hwy 135 to Main St.

 **ICEBOX DAYS**

Description:	This week-long celebration includes snow sculpture contests, turkey bowling, snowshoe racing, 5K and 10K runs, a bonfire, dart 8 ball and bridge tournaments.
Occurrence:	Third week in January
Write to:	International Falls Area Chamber of Commerce, 301 2nd Ave, International Falls, MN 56649
Phone:	218.283.9400 or 800.FALLS.MN (800.325.5766)
Website:	www.intlfalls.org/icebox.htm#top
Directions:	Take I-35 to Duluth and Hwy 53 N out of Duluth to International Falls. Events take place downtown.

 **JUDY GARLAND FESTIVAL**

Description:	This festival is for *The Wizard of Oz* fans to take in big-screen film showings, seminars, Q & A sessions, live performances, even mingle with the Munchkins, while kids' can participate in their own activities. Guest celebrities have included Mickey Rooney, June Allyson and Margaret O'Brien.
Occurrence:	Last weekend in June, 10 am–5 pm Th–Sa
Write to:	2727 Hwy 169 S, PO Box 724, Grand Rapids, MN 55744
Phone:	218.327.9276 or 800.664.JUDY (800.664.5839)
E-mail:	jgarland@uslink.net
Website:	www.judygarlandmuseum.com
Directions:	The Garland Museum is across from Home Depot on Hwy 169 S, two mi. from Hwy 2 in Grand Rapids.

 **RANIER SUMMER FESTIVAL**

Description:	This annual festival offers a family street dance, a sailing regatta, music on the boardwalk, art exhibits, plenty of food and a traditional powwow.
Occurrence:	August
Write to:	International Falls Area Chamber of Commerce, 301 2nd Ave, International Falls, MN 56649
Phone:	218.286.5699 or 800.FALLS.MN (800.325.5766)

Directions:	Take I-35 to Duluth and Hwy 53 N out of Duluth to International Falls. Festival is three mi. E of town on Hwy 11.

 ## TALL TIMBER DAYS

Description:	Relive the days of a bygone era and join in the fun and festivities that celebrate Grand Rapids' logging heritage. Enjoy a parade, crafts, contests, chainsaw demonstrations, street games for kids, a lumberjack show and wood carving.
Occurrence:	First weekend in August
Cost:	Free
Write to:	Tall Timber Days, PO Box 134, Grand Rapids, MN 55744
Phone:	218.326.6431 or 218.326.5618
Directions:	Downtown Grand Rapids at Central School.

 ## VOYAGEUR WINTER FESTIVAL

Description:	Ely's Voyageur Winter Festival is 11 days filled with fun activities for the entire family, including an opening ceremony, Snow Sculpture Symposium, Mukluk Ball, craft fair, kids' art fair, sled dog races and wilderness trek ski races.
Occurrence:	End of January–beginning of February
Write to:	Ely Chamber of Commerce, 1600 E Sheridan St, Ely, MN 55731
Phone/Fax:	Ph: 218.365.6123 or 800.777.7281; Fax: 218.365.5929
E-mail:	SIS2wolf@aol.com
Website:	www.voyageurwinterfestival.com
Directions:	260 mi. N of Minneapolis/St. Paul; 110 mi. NE of Duluth. Follow Hwy 53 N from Duluth to Hwy 169 N of Virginia. Hwy 169 will take you right into Ely.

COUNTIES INCLUDED IN THIS SECTION:

CARLTON COUNTY was established in 1857. It was named for Rueben Carlton, an early settler and an original Minnesota State Senate member. The county seat is Carlton. The area is 845 square miles which ranks 27th in the state. Population is 31,671 people, which ranks 31st in Minnesota. Population density is 36.8 people per square mile, which ranks 35th in the state.

COOK COUNTY was established in 1874. It was named for Major Michael Cook, a territorial and state senator who also served in the army during the Civil War. The county seat is Grand Marais. The area is 3,340 square miles, which ranks 2nd in the state. Population is 5,168 people, which ranks 84th in Minnesota. Population density is 3.6 people per square mile, which ranks 86th in the state.

ITASCA COUNTY was established in 1857. It was named through the combination of the Latin words for "truth" and "head," contrived by Henry Schoolcraft. The county seat is Grand Rapids. The area is 2,928 square miles, which ranks 6th in the state. Population is 43,992 people, which ranks 20th in Minnesota. Population density is 16.5 people per square mile, which ranks 62nd in the state.

KOOCHICHING COUNTY was established in 1906. This Cree word is thought to refer to the mist off of the falls where Rainy Lake flows into Rainy River. The county seat is International Falls. The area is 3,154 square miles, which ranks 3rd in the state. Population is 14,355 people, which ranks 59th in Minnesota. Population density is 4.6 people per square mile, which ranks 85th in the state.

LAKE COUNTY was established in 1856. It was named for its boundary with Lake Superior. The county seat is Two Harbors. The area is 2,991 square miles, which ranks 5th in the state. Population is 11,058 people, which ranks 69th in Minnesota. Population density is 5.3 people per square mile, which ranks 83rd in the state.

ST. LOUIS COUNTY was established in 1855. It was named for the St. Louis River, which is the largest river flowing into Lake Superior. The county seat is Duluth. The area is 6,860 square miles, which ranks 1st in the state. Population is 200,528 people, which ranks 6th in Minnesota. Population density is 32.2 people per square mile, which ranks 38th in the state.

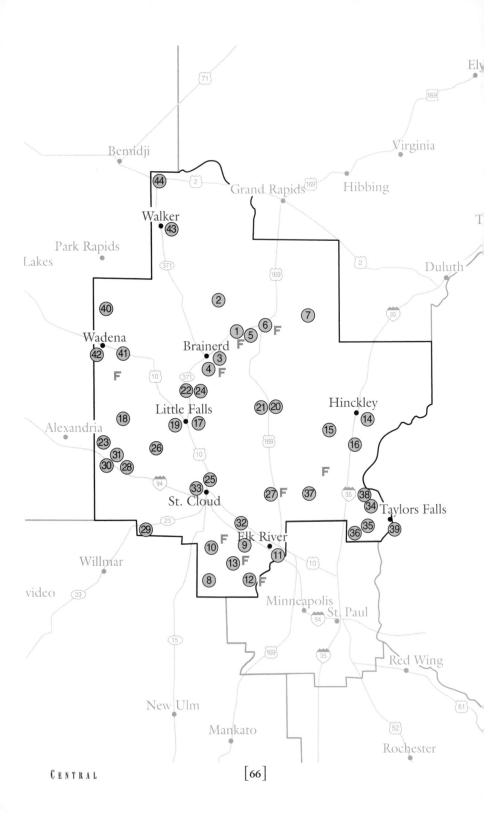

CENTRAL MINNESOTA

ATTRACTIONS WITHIN AN HOUR'S DRIVE OF:

(#) = historic sites   **F** = festivals

Listings in grey print are found in other sections but are within an hour's drive of the city.

CROFT MINE HISTORICAL PARK

① Description: Located on the former Croft Mine, this site is full of iron ore history. Visitors will enjoy a surprisingly realistic simulated ride down a mine shaft and many other mining exhibits and artifacts. Also on site is a library, theater, gift shop and a lovely picnic area.

Seasons/Hours: Memorial Day–Labor Day: 11 am–5 pm daily; other times by appointment

Cost: Adults: $5.50, students and seniors: $4.50, children under kindergarten age: free

Address: Hwy 6 N, Crosby, MN 56455

Phone: 218.546.5466

Directions: From downtown Crosby go N on Hwy 6.

CROSSLAKE AREA HISTORICAL SOCIETY

② Description: Find a replicated log village including a general store, homestead, schoolhouse, cottage, saloon, and loggers' camp. Also, visit the original town hall and check out summer events such as Musicfest and the Candlelight Tour.

Seasons/Hours: Memorial Day–Labor Day: 11 am–4 pm Sa–Su

Cost: Free, varied costs for special events

Address: PO Box 134, Crosslake, MN 56442

Phone/Fax: Ph: 218.692.4056; Fax: 218.692.5400

Directions: From Cross Lake, follow Hwy 66 N.

CROW WING COUNTY HISTORICAL SOCIETY MUSEUM

③ Description Located in the old county jail house and sheriff's residence, this museum depicts life at the turn of the century in the Brainerd area. There is a special display that chronicles the Milford Mine disaster of 1924, in addition to the exhibits featuring artifacts from Native Americans, the lumber industry, woodworking tools, crafts, textiles, household goods and farming implements. A gift shop is available with books and other items.

Seasons/Hours: Memorial Day–Labor Day: 10 am–4 pm M–F; closed Sa–Su; Labor Day–Memorial Day: 1 pm–5 pm Tu–F; 10 am–2 pm Sa

Cost: $3 donations suggested

Address:	320 Laurel Ave, Box 722, Brainerd, MN 56401
Phone/Fax:	Ph: 218.829.3268; Fax: 218.828.4434
E-mail:	history@brainerd.net
Directions:	From Hwy 371 and Laurel Ave go W two blocks.

CROW WING STATE PARK

④ *Description:*	Explore the trails the ox carts took between St. Paul and the Red River settlements when trade ran the surrounding area. Visitors can enjoy hiking, camping, fishing and canoeing on the Mississippi River. See the view from the Chippewa lookout. Visit the oldest house north of St. Anthony Falls, the Beaulieu House, or walk the boardwalk that runs through the old Crow Wing town.
Seasons/Hours:	Year-round: 9 am–4 pm Su–Th; 9 am–9 pm F–Sa
Cost:	Day pass $7; annual pass $25
Address:	3124 State Park Rd., Brainerd, MN 56401
Phone/Fax:	Ph: 218.825.3075; Fax: (866) 857.2757
Website:	www.dnr.state.mn.us/state_parks/crow_wing; for reservations: www.stayatmnparks.com
Directions:	On 371 S of Brainerd. Head W on Cty Rd 27. Watch for signs.

TRIVIA Minnesota is home to well over 6,000 state and federal campsites.

CUYUNA RANGE HISTORICAL MUSEUM

⑤ *Description:*	Focusing on the areas early mining history, this museum is home to some wonderful displays of the way life was at home and in the mine. Also on display is the rock collection of range founder Cuyler Adams.
Seasons/Hours:	June–Labor Day: 10 am–4 pm M–F; or by appointment
Cost:	Free
Address:	101 1st St NE, Soo Line Depot, Crosby, MN 56441
Phone:	218.546.6178
Directions:	Located one block N of Main St on Hallet Ave in Crosby.

DEPOT AND LOG MUSEUMS

⑥ **Description:** With two separate museums, this site is definitely worth checking out. The 1916 train depot is home to many exhibits which explore the railroad and lumber industries. This is also the building where the gift shop and research facilities can be found. The second museum is a replica of an old logging camp, complete with a black smith shop and dining hall.

Seasons/Hours: Depot Museum: Sept–May: 10 am–4:30 pm W, F & Sa; Depot and Log Museum: Apr–Oct: 10 am–4:30 pm W, F & Sa; or by appointment

Cost: Free

Address: PO Box 215, Aitkin, MN 56431

Phone: 218.927.3348

E-mail: achs@mlecmn.net

Website: www.aitkin.com/achs

Directions: Located in the city of Aitkin two blocks S of the stoplights at the junction of Hwy 169 and Hwy 210.

Don't miss this: Depot and Log Museum Gift Shop: the museum store offers gifts and publications pertaining to the area's history.

SAVANNA PORTAGE STATE PARK

⑦ **Description:** Come retrace the steps the Native Americans and voyageurs took along the Savanna Portage Trail. Visitors to the park can enjoy the 15,818 acres worth of hiking and biking on the trails, swimming in Loon Lake and fishing on the continental divide. When the snows come there are 10 miles of trails for cross-country skiers and 60 miles of trails designated for snowmobiling.

Seasons/Hours: Year-round: 9 am–4 pm Su–Th; 9 am–9 pm F–Sa; call ahead for winter hours

Cost: Call park for fees

Address: 55626 Lake Place, McGregor, MN 55760

Phone/Fax: Ph: 218.426.3271; Fax: 218.426.4437

Website: www.dnr.state.mn.us/state_parks/savanna_portage

Directions: Hwy 65 N to Aitkin Cty Rd 14, follow for 11 miles to the park.

Forests cover 16,718,000 acres of land in Minnesota, which accounts for 35 percent of the state.

COKATO MUSEUM AND GUST AKERLUND STUDIO

⑧ Description: This local museum concentrates on the history of Cokato and the surrounding area. There is a 1905 display of a camera studio of that time period. It still contains original furnishings and equipment. Also there is a reconstructed log cabin, sauna, and a street from Cokato from 1900.

Seasons/Hours: Year-round: 9 am–4:30 pm Tu–F; 10 am–4 pm Sa; 12 pm–4 pm Su; May–Oct: open M; tours by appointment; closed holidays

Cost: Free

Address: 175 4th St W, Cokato, MN 55321

Phone/Fax: Ph: 320.286.2427; Fax: 320.286.5876

E-mail: cokatomuseum@cmgate.com

Website: www.cokato.mn.us/cmhs/

Directions: In Cokato from Hwy 12, turn S on Broadway for three blocks, then W at 4th St.

LITTLE MOUNTAIN SETTLEMENT MUSEUM

⑨ Description: The Little Mountain Settlement Museum is dedicated to the immigrants from Norway, Germany, England, Sweden, Ireland and Scotland. There are three log buildings that contain furnishings typical to the period. Visitors can explore a schoolhouse, firehouse, sleigh shed, ropemakers shop and craft shop.

Seasons/Hours: May–Oct 1: 1 pm–5 pm Sa-Su

Cost: Free

Address: Box 581, Territorial Road, Monticello, MN 55362

Phone/Fax: Ph: 763.295.2950

Directions: Located in Monticello just off Broadway at 4th and Washington.

MINNESOTA PIONEER PARK

⑩ Description: This fantastic seven-acre site has 24 buildings and thousands of artifacts. Stroll down the boardwalk of a replica of a typical Main Street in Central Minnesota and imagine life in the 1890s. The park includes a 1902 house (part log cabin), an 1886 Finnish Apostolic church with unique flooring, an embossed tin interior, tin exterior, the original 1887 Annandale Train Depot with a Soo Line caboose, and a buggy and harness shop. Also find one of only 14 historical mortuaries in the country. The gift shop is located in the Train Depot. This park also provides living history day camps for youth in elementary or middle school the summers.

Seasons/Hours: Memorial Day–Labor Day: 10 am–4 pm Tu–F; 1 pm–5 pm Sa–Su; check for special seasonal activities

Cost: Adults: $5, seniors 60 and up: $4, youth 6–16: $3, children 5 and under: free

Address: 725 Pioneer Park Trl, Hwy 55, Annandale, MN 55302

Phone/Fax: Ph: 320.274.8489; Fax: 320.274.9612

E-mail: pioneerp@lakedalelink.net

Website: www.pioneerpark.org/

Directions: Located at the eastern edge of Annandale on Hwy 55.

OLIVER H. KELLEY FARM

⑪ Description: Step back in time at this truly authentic hands-on mid-1800s farm. Costumed guides can be found all over the grounds going about the daily farm chores. Picking vegetables, churning butter, pumping water, baking bread and caring for animals are just a few things guests are invited to do at this living history site.

Seasons/Hours: Mid-April–May and Sept–Oct: educational and group tours by appointment; Memorial Day–Labor Day: 10 am–5 pm M, Th–Sa; 12 pm–5 pm Su; Sept: 10 am–5 pm Sa; 12 pm–5 pm Su

Tim Rummelhoff, courtesy Minnesota Historical Society

Oliver H. Kelley Farm

Cost:	Adults: $7, seniors: $6, children 6–12: $4, children under 5: free
Address:	15788 Kelley Farm Rd., Elk River, MN 55330
Phone:	763.441.6896
E-mail:	kelleyfarm@mnhs.org
Website:	www.mnhs.org/places/sites/ohkf/
Directions:	Two mi. SE of Elk River on Hwy 10 and Hwy 169.

ROCKFORD AREA HISTORICAL SOCIETY

⑫ *Description:*	This house was built in the 1880 by George Ames who was one of the founding fathers of Rockford. The house was donated to the City of Rockford in 1984. The house has been furnished with items belonging to all three families depicting each time period. Genealogy research is available. One-hour guided tours for school trips and home schooling are encouraged.
Seasons/Hours:	Memorial Day–Labor Day: Tu 11 am–2 pm; Th 4 pm–7 pm; or by appointment; call for special events
Cost:	Adults: $5, youth 6–15: $3, children under 6: free
Address:	8136 Bridge St, Rockford, MN 55373
Phone:	763.477.5383
E-mail:	rahs@uninternet.com
Website:	www.cityofrockford.org/storkhouse/index.htm
Directions:	In Rockford, go one block off Hwy 55 on the Crow River.

WRIGHT COUNTY HISTORICAL SOCIETY AND HERITAGE CENTER

⑬ *Description:*	Among of the exhibits at the Wright County Heritage Center is the *Nelsonian*, a 32-piece one-man-band designed and built by Albert Nelson and was part of the 1933 World's Fair held in Chicago. Hubert H. Humphrey's 1926 Ford Model T is on exhibit with a collection of his campaign memorabilia and information. A log cabin and the ca. 1908 Chatham Town Hall buildings are also on the property. The archives and reference library houses information and materials made available for researching local and family history.
Seasons/Hours:	June–Sept: 8 am–4:30 pm Tu–F; 8 am–4 pm Sa; Oct–May 8 am–4:30 pm M–F
Cost:	Free
Address:	2001 N Hwy 25, Buffalo, MN 55303

Phone:	763.682.7323
Directions:	Located in Buffalo on Hwy 25 just eight mi. S of I-94, or 2½ mi. N of Hwy 55.

 The geographical shape of Wright County is a truncated version of the shape of the state of Minnesota.

HINCKLEY FIRE MUSEUM

⑭ *Description:*	On September 1, 1894, one of the worst forest fires in history destroyed 400 square miles of pine forest, burned six villages to the ground and killed 418 people in four hours. This museum which was the St. Paul and Duluth Railroad Depot—rebuilt immediately after the fire—is now on the National Register of Historic Places. It offers a children's exhibit, video documentary, stories and exhibits about the catastrophic fire, in addition to displays depicting the logging and farming way of life.
Seasons/Hours:	May 1–mid-Oct: 10 am–5 pm Tu–Sa; 12 pm–5 pm Su; school tours by appointment
Cost:	Adults: $5, seniors: $4, youth 13–18: $2, children 6–12: $1
Address:	106 Old Hwy 61, PO Box 40, Hinckley, MN 55037
Phone:	320.384.7338
E-mail:	hfire@ecenet.com
Directions:	Exit I-35 at Hinckley and go W on Fire Monument Rd. Take a right on Old Hwy 61, go three blocks and follow the signs.

 The height of the 1894 Hinckley Fire reached an estimated 4½ miles high. Sightings of the fire were reported as far away as Mason City, IA.

KANABEC COUNTY HISTORICAL SOCIETY

⑮ *Description:*	Home to three schoolhouses and surrounded by 37 acres, this site offers plenty of nature trails, picnic spots and play areas in addition to their many fine buildings. The history center's main building houses an art gallery and research library, which includes an archive of Kanabec County newspapers dating back

to 1884. Exhibits change throughout the year. Be sure to check out their gift shop featuring many local handcrafts.

Seasons/Hours:	10 am–4:30 pm M–Sa; 12:30 pm–4:30 pm Su & holidays
Cost:	Adults: $3, students K–12: $1, family: $8, preschool and members: free
Address:	805 W Forest Ave, PO Box 113, Mora, MN 55051
Phone/Fax:	Ph: 320.679.1665; Fax: 320.679.1673
E-mail:	center@kanabechistory.org
Website:	www.kanabechistory.org
Directions:	In Mora turn W on W Forest Ave to the Kanabec History Center.

 TRIVIA Mora, MN, the sister city to Mora, Sweden, has the largest Dala Horse in the US.

NORTH WEST COMPANY FUR POST

⑯ *Description:*	Follow costumed guides through this re-created trading post. Visitors will learn about how trade operated between the Europeans and the Ojibwe in 1804. Pack a picnic and enjoy the mile and a half worth of trails along Snake River.
Seasons/Hours:	May–Labor Day: 10 am–5 pm M–Sa; 12 pm–5 pm Su; Labor Day–October 31st: 10 am–5 pm F–Sa; 12pm–5 pm Su
Cost:	Adults: $7, seniors: $6, children 6–12: $4, children 6 and under and MHS members: free
Address:	PO Box 51, Pine City, MN 55063
Phone:	320.629.6356
E-mail:	nwcfp@mnhs.org

Minnesota Historical Society

North West Company Fur Post

Website:	www.mnhs.org/places/sites/nwcfp/
Directions:	From I-35, take Exit 169 at Pine City and go W 1½ mi. on Hwy 7. The building is on the right.

CHARLES A. LINDBERGH HOUSE

(17) *Description:*   Take a tour of the childhood home of world renowned aviator Charles A. Lindbergh. Many original furnishings and family possessions are still intact. Explore the full-scale replica of the cockpit from *The Spirit of St. Louis*, the plane he flew on his historic flight across the Atlantic Ocean. See the Volkswagen Beetle that Lindbergh drove on four continents, watch vintage footage of his historic flight and follow in Lindbergh's youthful footsteps along trails by the Mississippi.

Minnesota Historical Society

Charles A. Lindbergh House

Seasons/Hours:	Memorial Day–Labor Day: 10 am–5 pm M–Sa; 12 pm–5 pm Su; Labor Day–late Oct: 10 am–4 pm Sa; 12 pm–4 pm Su
Cost:	Adults: $7, seniors: $6, children 6–12: $4, children under 6 or MHS members: free
Address:	1620 Lindbergh Dr S, Little Falls, MN 56345
Phone:	320.632.3154; 888.PAST.FUN (888.727.8386)
E-mail:	lindbergh@mnhs.org
Website:	www.mnhs.org/places/sites/lh/
Directions:	The house is across the street from the Charles A. Lindbergh State Park, located two mi. S of Little Falls on the western side of the Mississippi River.

CHARLES A. WEYERHAEUSER MEMORIAL MUSEUM

⑱ Description: The museum, owned by the Morrison County Historical Society, has two permanent exhibit rooms and a rotating display dedicated to county history. Topics include logging industry, past county residents, Ojibwe life and natural history. The museum also features extensive research resources for genealogy and other county history. Tours are self-guided. The site includes a small gift shop with select history books and souvenirs.

Seasons/Hours: Year-round: 10 am–5 pm Tu–Sa; summer: 1 pm–5 pm Su; guided tours by request

Cost: Free

Address: 2151 Lindbergh Dr S, PO Box 239, Little Falls, MN 56345

Phone: 320.632.4007

E-mail: mchs@littlefalls.net

Website: www.morrisoncountyhistory.org

Directions: Go approximately two mi. S of Hwy 27 on Lindbergh Dr S past the Lindbergh House in Little Falls.

TRIVIA In 1861 Minnesota was the first state to offer troops for the Union army at the outbreak of the Civil War.

CHRISTIE HOME MUSEUM

⑲ Description: This Victorian Queen Anne home was built in 1901 by Dr. George Christie and his wife Susan. Some special features of the interior of the house are stained glass windows, Tiffany globes, prism-cut plate glass in window lights and a collection of 1550 books. Also on site is an elaborately furnished carriage house.

Seasons/Hours: June–Aug: 1:30 pm–4:30 pm W–Su

Cost: Adults: $5; students: $3

Address: 15 Central Ave, Long Prairie, MN 56347

E-mail: lpchambr@rea-alp.com

Website: www.longprairie.org/attractions.htm

Directions: From Hwy 71 in Long Prairie, go one block E on Central Ave. The Christie Home is on the corner of 1st St and Central Ave.

KATHIO STATE PARK

(20) Description: With over 30 identified archaeological sites, this park holds over 9,000 years of human history. In addition to camping, hiking, fishing, boating and swimming, visitors are invited to observe the wildlife from the park's 100-foot fire tower.

Seasons/Hours: Year-round: park: 8 am–10 pm daily; office: 9 am–9 pm daily

Cost: State park permit: $25; day-use sticker: $7; camping fees: $11–$18

Address: 15066 Kathio State Park Rd., Onamia, MN 56359-2207

Phone: 320.532.3523

Directions: Go to mile post marker #221 on Hwy 169, about eight mi. N of Onamia. Watch for the Kathio Arrowhead sign and take Cty Rd 26 for about one mi. to the park entrance.

MILLE LACS INDIAN MUSEUM

Mille Lacs Indian Museum

Minnesota Historical Society

(21) Description: Learn about the Mille Lacs band of Ojibwe from yesterday and today through the many exhibits, displays and demonstrations available at the museum. Take a guided tour through the Four Seasons Room with its life size diorama depicting the traditional activities that occurred during each season. Next door is a 1930s trading post which now houses the museum store, full of hand-crafted gifts by Mille Lacs artisans. Check website for special workshops offered monthly.

Seasons/Hours: Memorial Day–Labor Day: 10 am–6 pm daily; May–Sept: 11 am–4 pm F–M; open off-season for groups and tours by appointment

Cost: Adults: $7, seniors: $6, children ages 6–12: $4; children 6 and under and MHS members: free; special group and education rates available

Address:	43411 Oodena Dr, Onamia, MN 56359
Phone:	320.532.3632
E-mail:	millelacs@mnhs.org
Website:	www.mnhs.org/millelacs
Directions:	The museum is on Hwy 169 on the SW shore of Lake Mille Lacs, eight mi. S of Garrison or 12 mi. N of Onamia.

 Lake Mille Lacs covers about 200 square miles with a maximum depth of 84 feet.

MINNESOTA MILITARY MUSEUM

㉒ *Description:*	The exhibits at the museum follow Minnesota's military history from the era of the frontier to the Gulf War. Inside you will find vehicles, weapons, uniforms and photographs, visitors are even invited to try uniforms and helmets on. Outside tanks, helicopters and planes are on display. Be sure to check out the museum's gift shop where among other things, personalized dog tags are available for purchase.
Seasons/Hours:	June 1–Aug 31: 10 am–5 pm daily; Sept. 1–May 31: 9 am–4 pm Th–F
Cost:	$3 donation suggested for non-military adults
Address:	15000 Hwy 115, Camp Ripley, Little Falls, MN 56345
Phone:	320.632.7374
E-mail:	mnmuseum@brainerd.net
Website:	www.dma.state.mn.us/cpripley/SpecFeatures/muse1.htm
Directions:	Go approximately 25 mi. S of Brainerd on Hwy 371, or seven mi. N of Little Falls on Hwy 115.

 The brown bat can eat 500 mosquitoes in an hour.

OSAKIS AREA HERITAGE CENTER

㉓ Description: Osakis itself is located on the historic Red River Ox Cart Trail and 6,300-acre Lake Osakis. This small center which specializes in the history of Douglas and Todd counties holds family files, old pictures and artifacts. Check out the Herberger Memorial Flower Garden which evolves yearly, and an authentic log cabin

Seasons/Hours: Year-round: 9 am–5 pm M–F; additionally in summer: 10 am–2 pm Sa

Cost: Free

Write to: PO Box 327, Osakis, MN 56360

Phone: 320.859.3777

E-mail: history@lakeosakis.com

Website: www.lakeosakismn.com/history.html

Directions: Approximately 120 mi. NW of Minneapolis/St. Paul off I-94, at the intersection of Hwy 127 and Hwy 27, on the eastern edge of Osakis.

 Osakis is home to the original Herberger's Department Store, owned and managed by founder George Herberger from 1890 to 1956.

TODD COUNTY HISTORICAL MUSEUM

㉔ Description: After a stint in the 1929 log cabin at the Todd County Fairgrounds, the Historical Society Museum moved to its present location in the Hart Press building. The museum offers the visitors artifacts of Todd County and murals showing life in the 1800s and 1900s. The historical society also has an in-depth research center.

Seasons/Hours: Year-round: 10 am–4 pm M–F; 1 pm–4 pm Sa (Sa: May–Labor Day only)

Cost: Fee for museum and research; free to members

Address: 333 Central Ave, PO Box 146, Long Prairie, MN 56347

Phone: 320.732.4426

Directions: Across the street from the Post Office on Central Ave, downtown Long Prairie.

Don't miss this:	Todd County was the site of the Winnebago Agency which was located in Long Prairie from 1846 to 1855. An historic marker at the corner of Central Ave and 3rd St in downtown Long Prairie denotes the site of the Agency.

BENTON COUNTY HISTORICAL SOCIETY

㉕ *Description:*	This society holds probate records, surname files, cemetery records, newspaper microfilm dating back to the early 1800s. Find information on townships and cities in the county, as well as many displays in the museum.
Seasons/Hours:	April–Aug: 10 am–3 pm M–Th; Sept–Mar: 10 am–3 pm Tu–Th; 10 am–3 pm on the 2nd Sa of the month
Cost:	Free, donations accepted
Address:	218 1st St N, PO Box 426, Sauk Rapids, MN 56379
Phone:	320.253.9614
E–mail:	bchsmus@cloudnet.com
Website:	www.members.aol.com/bchsmus
Directions:	From Hwy 15, exit on Benton Dr to 1st St N.

BORGSTROM HOUSE MUSEUM

㉖ *Description:*	This 1913 house was donated by Axel and Carrie Borgstrom in order for the community to preserve the history of the Upsala area. There are ten rooms portraying the Borstrom's Swedish heritage, as well as much of Upsala's history and artifacts of state and local interest. The town's 1928 Reo Firetruck has also been preserved, courtesy of the Upsala Area Historical Society.
Seasons/Hours:	By appointment
Cost:	Donations appreciated
Address:	113 Birch Ave, Upsala, MN 56384
Write to:	Upsala Area Historical Society, Box 35, Upsala, MN 56384
Phone:	320.573.2335
Website:	www.upsala.k12.mn.us/uahs
Directions:	Just off of Hwy 238 on Birch Ave in Upsala.

MELROSE AREA MUSEUM

㉗ Description: The museum has changing exhibits covering two floors. They feature kitchen utensils, office equipment, railroad, agriculture, art, fashion, business and children's toys. There is a medical room and a room with military gear. The museum also contains a large collection of Charles A. Lindbergh memorabilia.

Seasons/Hours: Year-round: 9 am–12 pm & 1 p.m–4 pm W; other times by appointment

Cost: Adults: $2, children 9–15: $1; children under 9 and members: free; family: $5 (suggested donations)

Address: 518 E 2nd St S, Melrose, MN 56352

Phone: Ph: (30) 256.4996

Website: www.melrosemnhistory.com

Directions: Located in Melrose off I-94. Turn right on 2nd St, follow signs.

MILLE LACS COUNTY HISTORICAL SOCIETY DEPOT MUSEUM

㉘ Description: The museum is located in the Great Northern Depot Building, which was built in 1902. The 1856 Princeton School District No. 1 Schoolhouse, the first in the county, hosts a yearly "pioneer school." Other attractions include a rare 1924 Wilcox water truck which was the first motorized firetruck used in Princeton. Exhibits include those depicting commercial trade, lumber industry, brick industry and agriculture in the Princeton area. The museum also specializes in genealogical research.

Seasons/Hours: Year-round: 11 am–4 pm W–Sa

Cost: Free, but donation appreciated

Address: 101 10th Ave S, Princeton, MN 55371

Phone: 763.389.1296

Directions: Hwy 169 to Hwy 95 E. Turn S on Rum River St to 1st St, then W to 10th Ave.

PAYNESVILLE HISTORICAL MUSEUM

㉙ Description: With an antique kitchen, pioneer schoolhouse and blacksmith shop, this museum also offers special exhibits featuring a collection of medical equipment, farming tools and toys. Genealogical and family history research is also available.

Seasons/Hours:	June–Aug: 10 am–4 pm Tu–Sa; 1 pm–4 pm Su
Cost:	Adults: $2; students: $1
Address:	251 Ampe Dr, Paynesville, MN 56362
Phone:	320.243.7547
Directions:	Located on the west side of Paynesville on Hwy 23.

SINCLAIR LEWIS
BOYHOOD HOME

③⓪ *Description:*	Enjoy a guided tour of the home—a National Historic Landmark and a Minnesota Historic Site—that inspired America's first Nobel Prize winner to write many of his books. This home was restored to the time when Harry Sinclair Lewis lived there with his parents and two brothers, which now features a wide collection of early twentieth century furnishings and a gift shop.
Seasons/Hours:	Memorial Day–Labor Day: 10 am–5 pm M–Sa; 11 am–5 pm Su; May and Sept: by appointment
Cost:	Adults: $4, seniors: $3, families: $8
Address:	812 Sinclair Lewis Ave, Sauk Centre, MN 56378
Phone:	320.352.5201
E-mail:	chamber@saukcentre.com
Directions:	In Sauk Centre, turn W at the stoplight at the Original Main St and Sinclair Lewis Ave and go three blocks.

SINCLAIR LEWIS
INTERPRETIVE CENTER

③① *Description:*	The Center is home to everything Sinclair, including his college diploma, his writing desk, Nobel Prize and even the urn that held his ashes. Visitors will also enjoy the "Birth of a Novel" exhibit that gives viewers a glimpse into Lewis' writing process.
Seasons/Hours:	Memorial Day–Labor Day: 8:30 am–5 pm M–F; 9 am–5 pm Sa–Su; Labor Day–Memorial Day: 8:30 am–4:30 pm M–F
Cost:	Free
Address:	1220 S Main St, Sauk Centre, MN 56378
Phone:	320.352.5201
E-mail:	chamber@saukcentre.com
Directions:	Located at the rest stop at the intersection of I-94 and Hwy 71 in Sauk Centre.

TRIVIA

In 1930 Sinclair Lewis became the first American to win a Nobel Peace Prize for literature.

SHERBURNE COUNTY HISTORICAL SOCIETY

㉜ **Description:** This building is home to an extensive collection of county records and over 5,000 photographs, as well as many rotating exhibits.

Sessons/Hours: Year-round: 8 am–5 pm M–F; 10 am–2 pm 1st & 3rd Sa of the month

Cost: Free

Address: 13122 1st St, Becker, MN 55308

Phone/Fax: Ph: 763.261.4433; Fax: 763.261.4437

E-mail: schs@sherbtel.net

Website: www.rootsweb.com/~mnschs/

Directions: In Becker located at intersection of Bradley Blvd and 1st St.

STEARNS COUNTY MUSEUM

㉝ **Description:** Any visitor to this museum can tell why it is hailed as one of the best in the state. This nationally accredited museum is home to a rare 1919 Pan automobile, a life-sized replica of a 1930s granite quarry, an 1880 barn and a walk-through replica of an 1850 natural environment. There is also an extensive research library specializing in German and Luxembourg immigration, a fabulous hands-on children's gallery and a Museum Store.

1919 Model A Pan Car

Seasons/Hours: Year-round: 10 am–4 pm M–Sa 12 pm–4 pm Su; closed holidays

Cost: Adults: $4, children: $2, children under 5: free; families: $10

Address: 235 S 33rd Ave, St. Cloud, MN 56301

Phone/Fax:	Ph: 320.253.8424 or toll free: (866) 253.8424; Fax: 320.253.2172
E-mail:	info@stearns-museum.org
Website:	www.stearns-museum.org
Directions:	In St. Cloud, go three blocks S of Division St (Hwy 23). From I-94, take Hwy 15 to 33rd Ave S, then to 2nd St S intersection.

 Minnesota's worst tornado claimed 74 lives on April 14, 1886 in the St. Cloud area.

AMADOR HERITAGE CENTER

㉞ *Description:*	The heritage center contains local artifacts and an 1865 Swedish log cabin that is being restored.
Seasons/Hours:	June–Sept: 1 pm–5 pm Su; tours by appointment summer weekends
Cost:	Donation
Address:	Maple St, Almelund, MN 55012
Write to:	15695 368th St, Almelund, MN 55012
Phone:	651.583.2883
E-mail:	lstrong@cornernet.com
Directions:	Located in Almelund, between Taylors Falls and North Branch on Hwy 95.

CHISAGO COUNTY HISTORY CENTER

㉟ *Description:*	Inside this 1900s Queen Anne house is extensive local history and genealogy research library, as well as a meeting room. The shelves are filled with a continually expanding collection of documentation on the history of the county and its pioneers, local events and cemetery burials.
Seasons/Hours:	Year-round: 10 am–3 pm M, W & F
Cost:	Library is free; nominal charge for meeting room
Address:	13100 3rd Ave N, PO Box 146, Lindstrom, MN 55045

Phone:	651.257.5310
Directions:	From Hwy 8 in Lindstrom, turn N on Olinda Trl. Go two blocks to the intersection of Olinda Trl and 3rd St.

GUSTAF'S HISTORIC HOUSE MUSEUM

㊱ *Description:*	Built in 1879 by Gustaf and Helena Anderson, this modest Italianate brick mansion is on the National Register of Historic Places. The Chisago County Historical Society plays host to community gatherings, educational programs and house tours and teas at the Gustaf's Historic House. For a unique experience, visitors have the option of staying the night at this bed and breakfast.
Seasons/Hours:	Year-round: 9 am–3 pm M, W–F
Cost:	Tours: $3 per person; other events vary
Address:	13045 Lake Blvd (US Hwy 8), PO Box 146, Lindstrom, MN 55045
Phone:	651.257.5310
Directions:	From I-35, take US Hwy 8 E to Lindstrom.

ISANTI COUNTY HISTORICAL SOCIETY

㊲ *Description:*	Located in the Heritage Center, facilities include a museum and genealogical research area. The society also maintains three sites listed on the National Register of Historic Places: West Riverside School which is the site of Old Time School, St. John's Lutheran Church which holds services throughout the year, and Spencer Brook School.
	West Riverside School is used for five weeks every summer for Old Time School, where children grades 1–8 spend a week in the life of a pioneer student. Dressing the part, these children play the games, read the books and sing the songs their turn-of-the-century counterparts once did. On the same grounds are the Edblad log cabin and a small blacksmith shop. This cabin is used for three weeks each summer for students K–8 to learn Swedish and Norwegian language and culture through games, crafts, songs and cooking.
Seasons/Hours:	9 am–3:30 pm M, Tu & Th; 9 a.m–1 pm Sa; other times by appointment
Cost:	Free, donations appreciated; nominal fees for research
Address:	33525 Flanders St, PO Box 525, Cambridge, MN 55008

Phone:	763.689.4229
E-mail:	generalICHS@nsatel.com
Website:	www.ICHS.ws
Directions:	From Cambridge, take Hwy 95 E to Flanders St and take a left. Follow the signs.

KARL OSKAR HOUSE

(38) *Description:* Based on the writings of Swedish author Vilhelm Moberg, the fictional characters of Karl and Kristina Oskar represent the struggles and experiences that many immigrants faced. A house much like one they might have lived in was built to hold a Swedish heritage museum. See original artifacts brought over from Sweden like authentic kitchen tools, a cradle, and an organ.

Hours: Tours by appointment

Cost: Free; $1 donation suggested

Address: Kichi-Saga County Park, Glader Blvd, Lindstrom, MN 55045

Phone/Fax: Ph: 651.257.5855; Fax: 651.257.2519

E-mail: tomtegarden@citlink.net

Directions: Located in the Kichi-Saga Park. From Hwy 8, go S on Cty Rd 25, then E on Glader Blvd to the park.

W.H.C. FOLSOM HOUSE MUSEUM

(39) *Description:* Built in 1855 by lumber baron and state legislature W.H.C. Folsom, this New England-style frame house was home to five generations of Folsoms. Tours are lead by knowledgeable volunteers and run on a continuous loop throughout the afternoon.

Seasons/Hours: Late May–mid-Oct: 1 pm–4:30 pm daily except Tu; group tours by appointment; open the first two weekends after Thanksgiving

Cost: Adults: $4, children ages 6–12: $1; MHS members: free

Address: 272 W Government St, Taylors Falls, MN 55084

Phone:	651.465.3125
E-mail:	folsomhouse@mnhs.org
Website:	www.mnhs.org/places/sites/fh/index.html
Directions:	Located in Taylors Falls, N of Hwy 8

PIONEER PARK

④⓪ *Description:*	Pioneer Park is located on the site of the first sawmill and the flourmill along the banks of the Red Eye River. In the park is a monument dedicated to the pioneers of the area. Behind the monument are three log buildings. There is an early rural log school, a pioneer barn and an early Finnish sauna. These buildings contain household, school, business and agricultural artifacts. Picnicking and camping facilities are also available in the park.
Seasons/Hours:	Memorial Day–Labor Day: 9 am–5 pm daily; park is open dawn–10 pm; guided tours call for appointment
Cost:	Free; fee for camping and rentals
Address:	US Hwy 71 S, Sebeka, MN 56477
Write to:	City of Sebeka, PO Box 305, Sebeka, MN 56477
Phone:	218.837.5773
E-mail:	cityofsebeka@wcta.net
Website:	City of Sebeka website is under construction
Directions:	Sebeka is located 14 mi. N of Wadena on Hwy 71. The park is right on Hwy 71.
Don't miss this:	See an 80-foot outdoor mural depicting the history of the area in downtown Sebeka.

VERNDALE HISTORICAL SOCIETY

④① *Description:*	Check out an exhibit on General McNair, artifacts and books published by the Historical Society about local people and the city. The museum is located in an old church.
Seasons/Hours:	By appointment
Cost:	Free
Address:	205 Brown St S, Verndale, MN 56481
Phone/Fax:	218.445.5309
Directions:	From Hwy 10, go two blocks N on Farwell St.

WADENA COUNTY HISTORICAL SOCIETY

④② Description: The museum has over 10,000 artifacts representing the many generations of residents the county has encountered, including a fascinating exhibit depicting weddings through the ages.

Seasons/Hours: Year-round: 9 am–3 pm Tu–F

Cost: Free

Address: 603 N Jefferson, Wadena, MN 56482

Phone: 218.631.9079

Directions: From Hwy 10, turn N on Hwy 71 and go four blocks. Located on the left side.

CASS COUNTY MUSEUM

④③ Description: The Cass County Museum features exhibits that pertain to the settlement of the county, such as logging, transportation and homesteading. The 1912 pioneer Huset School offers a hands-on experience of early country school days. An Ojibwe collection from the turn of the century includes birchbark canoes, stone tools and beadwork. The Historical Society Library offers extensive research materials, including photographs, newspapers, family histories and area publications.

Seasons/Hours: Memorial Day–Labor Day: 10 am–5 pm M–Sa

Cost: Adults: $3, children: $1, family (under 17): $6; nominal fees for research

Address: 201 Minnesota Ave W, Box 505, Walker, MN 56484

Phone: 218.547.7251 or 218.652. 4377 after hours

Directions: From the intersection of Hwy 34 and Hwy 371 in Walker, turn E on Minnesota Ave and go to 2nd St.

LYLE'S LOGGING CAMP AND MUSEUM

㊹ Description: Transformed from a Soo Line Depot, this museum offers a realistic look at life during the days when lumber was king. With audio tours available you can guide yourself through the bunkhouse, cookhouse and blacksmith shop. Visitors can also request a tour guide to get more in depth stories.

Seasons/Hours: May 15–Sept 15: 9 am–5 pm daily

Cost: Free

Address: Lyle Chisholm Drive, PO Box 548, Cass Lake, MN 56633

Phone: 218.335.6723

Directions: One block E at the junction of Hwy 371 and Hwy 2 in Cass Lake.

CENTRAL MINNESOTA FESTIVALS

LISTED ALPHABETICALLY

 ### ANNANDALE PIONEER FESTIVAL

Description:	Find treasures by local artisans, watch demonstrations, tour 23 buildings and sample delicious food.
Occurrence:	July
Cost:	Adults: $5, seniors: $4, children ages 6–16: $3, children 5 and under: free
Write to:	725 Pioneer Park Trl, Annandale, MN 55302
Phone:	320.274.8489
Directions:	From Buffalo, go 15 mi. on Hwy 55. From Howard Lake, go 15 mi. N on Wright Cty Rd 6 to Hwy 55. From Clearwater, go 20 mi. S of Clearwater on Hwy 24 to Hwy 55.

 ### BRAHAM PIE DAYS

Description:	Celebrating the Homemade Pie Capital of Minnesota, this festival includes pie related contests, craft fairs, entertainment and more.
Occurrence:	First Friday of August
Write to:	2nd Street Southwest, PO Box 383, Braham, MN 55006
Phone:	320.396-4956
Website:	www.braham.com
Directions:	From the Twin Cities, N 60 miles on Hwy 65 to E Hwy 107, follow to Freedom Park in downtown Braham.

BUFFALO DAYS CELEBRATION

Description:	Parade, fireworks, and carnival.
Occurrence:	June
Write to:	1472 10 St NW, Buffalo, MN 55313
Phone:	763.682.4444 ask for Joe
Directions:	25 mi. W of 494 and Hwy 55.

FESTIVAL OF ADVENTURERS AND WILLAM AITKIN FUR TRADE RENDEZVOUS

Description:	Come and witness what it was like to be in the pinery and lumber camps as well as what fur trade involved. Enjoy this festival of fun by taking a riverboat ride, enjoying music, games, food and fun.
Occurrence:	Second weekend in September
Write to:	Aitkin City Park, 24 3rd St NW, Aitkin, MN 56431
Phone/Fax:	Ph: 800.526.8342; Fax: 218.927.2316
E-mail:	upnorth@aitkin.com
Website:	www.aitkin.com/fest/fest.htm
Directions:	Located in the city park of Aitkin. The park is downtown just four blocks S of the only stoplight in Aitkin.

HERITAGE DAYS

Description:	The Heritage Days Festival in downtown Crosby offers events for the whole family, including The Cuyuna Country Critters Pet Show and the Serpent Lake Festival of Fine Arts. Various activities are offered by local merchants and organizations throughout the weekend. Saturday's events typically take place in Crosby Memorial Park.
Occurrence:	Third weekend in August (F–Su)
Write to:	The Crosby-Ironton Courier, PO Box 67, Crosby, MN 56441
Phone:	218.546.5029
E-mail:	courier@emily.net
Directions:	Events take place throughout downtown Crosby and in Crosby Memorial Park, which is one block off Main St.

OLD WADENA RENDEZVOUS

Description:	This rendezvous/folk festival is growing every year. Events include demonstrations like basketmaking, sculpture and canoe construction, Native American dance, storytelling and fur trapper reenactments. Experience life in Minnesota's past with music, food, art and lots of exciting exhibits.
Occurrence:	Held 2nd weekend in August; looking at a possible time in spring or fall to avoid the mosquitoes
Write to:	W.H.E.L.P., North Central Service Cooperative, 200 1st St NE, Staples, MN 56479
Phone:	W.H.E.L.P.: 218.894.1930 or Mr. Jamie Robertson: 218.631.4618
E-mail:	echo@echopress.com
Website:	www.mndestinations.com/wad_rendezvous.cfm
Directions:	Take State Hwy 10 to the Industrial Park/Tech College sign and turn N on Cty Rd 125; follow to 4-way stop and turn W on Cty Rd 2. Turn immediately N on Cty Rd 29 and follow to the brown Old Wadena sign on the right.

RAPIDS RIVER FOOD FEST

Description:	If you love food, you'll love the Rapids River Food Fest. With 25 food vendors, you'll have to try everything. Enjoy the music, games and entertainment for the whole family. Learn to fish, watch local firefighters have a water war and check out the stands selling homemade treasures. You're sure to have a ball!
Occurrence:	June
Write to:	Sauk Rapids City Hall, 115 2nd Avenue North, Sauk Rapids, MN 56379
Website:	www.ci.sauk-rapids.mn.us/
Directions:	On the east bank of the Mississippi River, 10th St N and River Ave N will bring you to Sauk Rapids' Municipal Park.

 ## RHYTHM OF THE RAILS

Description:	Enjoy a summer evening with romantic railroad lore and Brainerd area history through song, dance, melodrama, skits and music. Entertainment scheduled on Thursday, Friday, and

Saturday evenings the last three weekends in July. Fun for all ages.

Occurrence:	July
Cost:	Adults: $8, children under 14: $6
Write to:	303 Front St, Brainerd, MN 56401
Phone:	800.450.2838
E-mail:	jocro@brainerd.net
Directions:	Two blocks E of N 1st St and one block S of Hwy 210 in Brainerd on Front St.

ROCKFORD RIVER DAYS FESTIVAL

Description:	Rockford River Days Festival has live music available in the evenings and several activities are planned for each day. Some of these include a 10k run, river rafting race, a softball tournament and queen coronation. The Annual River Days Parade is always held on the last day of the festival in the afternoon. Come and join the fun.
Occurrence:	August
Write to:	6051 Terrace Circle, Rockford, MN 55373
Phone/Fax:	763.477.4261 ext. 2; Fax: 763.477.4393
E-mail:	rockford.river.days@juno.com
Directions:	This event takes place in the Riverside Park on the northern side of Main St along the Crow River.

RUM RIVER FESTIVAL

Description:	A parade, 5K run, craft fair, festival car show, pie and ice cream social, music, Little Britches Rodeo, street dance, airport brunch, speedway races and more.
Occurrence:	Second week in June
Write to:	705 2nd St N, Princeton, MN 55371
Phone/Fax:	Ph: 763.389.1764; Fax: 763.631.1764
E-mail:	pacc@sherbtel.net
Website:	www.rumriverfestival.com
Directions:	From St. Cloud take Hwy 23 E to Hwy 95 and go E to Princeton. Events happening around town.

COUNTIES INCLUDED IN THIS SECTION:

AITKIN COUNTY was established in 1857. It was named for William Alexander Aitkin who was an influential trader with the American Fur Company. The county seat is Aitkin. The area is 1,995 square miles, which ranks 10th in the state. Population is 15,301 people, which ranks 57th in Minnesota. Population density is 8.4 people per square mile, which ranks 80th in the state.

BENTON COUNTY was established in 1849. It was named for Thomas Hart Benton, a St. Louis senator who advocated free land laws which led to the development and growth of Minnesota. The county seat is Foley. The area is 413 square miles, which ranks 84th in the state. Population is 34,226 people, which ranks 26th in Minnesota. Population density is 83.8 people per square mile, which ranks 14th in the state.

CARVER COUNTY was established in 1855. It was named after Jonathan Carver, an explorer who made maps of the new frontier, documenting geography, numbers and locations of Indians and trade posts. The county seat is Chaska. The area is 376 square miles, which ranks 85th in the state. The population is 70,205 people, which ranks 11th in Minnesota. Population density is 196.6 people per square mile, which ranks 7th in the state.

CASS COUNTY was established in 1851. It was named for Lewis Cass, a statesman who commanded an expedition in 1820 from Detroit through Lake Huron, Lake Superior and into the upper Mississippi River. The county seat is Walker. The area is 2,414 square miles, which ranks 7th in the state. Population is 27,150 people, which ranks 36th in Minnesota. Population density is 13.5 people per square mile, which ranks 68th in the state.

CHISAGO COUNTY was established in 1851. Named for its largest lake, the word "Chisago" comes from the Chippewa name Ki-chi-sago meaning large and lovely. The county seat is Center City. The area is 442 square miles, which ranks 77th in the state. Population is 41,101 people, which ranks 22nd in Minnesota. Population density is 98.4 people per square mile, which ranks 13th in the state.

CROW WING COUNTY was established in 1857. It was named for a crow wing shaped island where the Crow Wing River and the Mississippi River join. The county seat is Brainerd. The area is 1,157 square miles, which ranks 17th in the state. Population is 55,099 people, which ranks 16th in Minnesota. Population density is 55.3 people per square mile, which ranks 23rd in the state.

ISANTI COUNTY was established in 1857. It was named after a former division of the Dakota who lived in the area surrounding the Rum River. The county seat is Cambridge. The area is 452 square miles, which ranks 74th in the state. Population is 31,287 people, which ranks 33rd in Minnesota. Population density is 71.3 people per square mile, which ranks 18th in the state.

KANABEC COUNTY was established in 1858. It was named after the Ojibwe word "snake" for the Snake River. The county seat is Mora. The area is 533 square miles, which ranks 66th in the state. Population is 14,996 people, which ranks 58th in Minnesota. Population density is 28.6 people per square mile, which ranks 42nd in the state.

MILLE LACS COUNTY was established in 1860. It was named for the French word meaning "thousand lakes." The county seat is Milaca. The area is 682 square miles, which ranks 47th in the state. Population is 22,330 people, which ranks 43rd in Minnesota. Population density is 38.9 people per square mile, which ranks 33rd in the state.

MORRISON COUNTY was established in 1856. It was named for William and Allen Morrison, both men were fur traders and traveled through the area of Lake Mille Macs. The county seat is Little Falls. The area is 1,153 square miles, which ranks 18th in the state.

Population is 31,712 people, which ranks 30th in Minnesota. Population density is 28.2 people per square mile, which ranks 43rd in the state.

PINE COUNTY was established in 1856. It was named for the extensive pine forests. The county seat is Pine City. The area is 1,435 square miles, which ranks 15th in the state. Population is 26,530 people, which ranks 38th in Minnesota. Population density is 18.8 people per square mile, which ranks 58th in the state.

SHERBURNE COUNTY was established in 1856. It was named for Moses Sherburne who was an associate justice of the Territorial Supreme Court and helped establish Minnesota law. The county seat is Elk River. The area is 451 square miles, which ranks 75th in the state. The population is 64,417 people, which ranks 12th in Minnesota. Population density is 147.6 people per square mile, which ranks 9th in the state.

STEARNS COUNTY was established in 1855. The county was intended to be named after Isaac I. Stevens but was rather misnamed after Charles T. Stearns. However, county residents did not object since Stearns was also a well-respected man. The county seat is St. Cloud. The area is 1,390 square miles which ranks 16th in the state. Population is 133,166 people, which ranks 7th in Minnesota. Population density is 99 people per square mile, which ranks 12th in the state.

TODD COUNTY was established in 1856. It was named after John Baines Smith Todd, a first cousin of Mary Todd Lincoln, and was commander of Fort Ripley at the time. The county seat is Long Prairie. The area is 979 square miles which ranks 24th in the state. Population is 24,426 people, which ranks 41st in Minnesota. Population density is 25.9 people per square mile, which ranks 46th in the state.

WADENA COUNTY was established in 1873. It was named for the Ojibwe Chief Wadena. The county seat is Wadena. The area is 543 square miles, which ranks 65th in the state. Population is 13,713 people, which ranks 60th in Minnesota. Population density is 25.6 people per square mile, which ranks 47th in the state.

WRIGHT COUNTY was established in 1855. It was named after Silas Wright, a politician and former US Senator from the state of New York. The county seat is Buffalo. The area is 714 square miles, which ranks 45th in the state. Population is 89,986 people, which ranks 9th in Minnesota. Population density is 136 people per square mile, which ranks 10th in the state.

NOTES

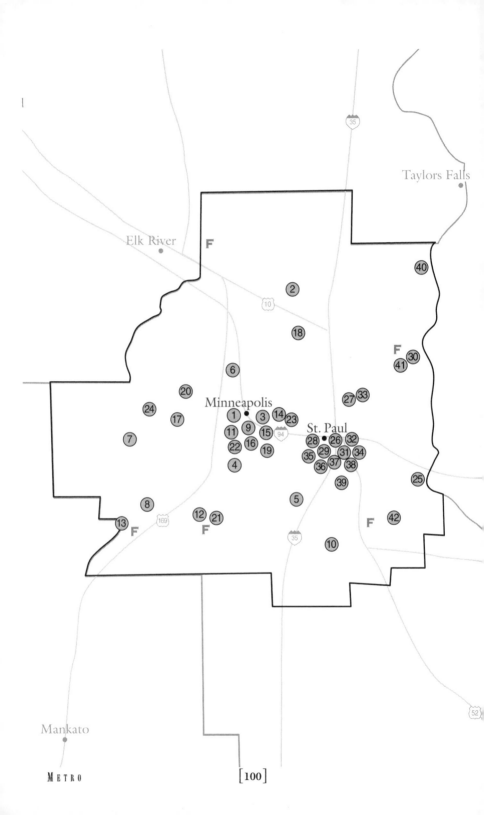

Taylors Falls

Elk River **F**

Minneapolis

St. Paul

Mankato

METRO

[100]

METRO AREA MINNESOTA

ATTRACTIONS WITHIN AN HOUR'S DRIVE OF:

(#) = historic sites   F = festivals

In addition to the these metro listings, many attractions in other sections of this book are within an hour's drive of some portions of the metro area (Central Section: Elk River, Taylors Falls, St. Cloud; Southwest Section: Mankato; Southeast Section: Red Wing, Rochester). Refer to the listings near these cities and consult a road map to determine a particular site's proximity.

AMERICAN SWEDISH INSTITUTE

① Description: The American Swedish Institute is located in the early twentieth century mansion of Swan Turnblad. It houses a collection of the family's possessions and donated items pertinent to Swedish heritage. There is a special exhibit about the Swedish immigration to the Twin Cities. Come and see the beauty of the Twin Cities' only castle.

Seasons/Hours: 12 pm–4 pm Tu, Th–Sa; 12 pm–8 pm W; 1 pm–5 pm Su; extended in Nov and Dec

Cost: Adults: $5, seniors ages 62 and up: $4, youth ages 6–18: $3, children 6 and under and members: free; everyone is free on the 1st W of each month

Address: 2600 Park Ave, Minneapolis, MN 55407

Phone/Fax: Ph: 612.871.4907; Fax: 612.871.8682

E-mail: info@americanswedishinst.org

Website: www.americanswedishinst.org/

Directions: Located five min. S of downtown on the corner of Park Ave and 26th St.

ANOKA COUNTY HISTORY CENTER AND LIBRARY

② Description: The Anoka County Historical Society was founded in 1934. The home of Anoka County History Center and Library is in the former Anoka City Library building. Visit and marvel at the architecture of the early 1960s, designed by the award-winning firm of Griswold & Rauma. The collections of artifacts include wedding gowns, logging equipment, quilts, a bison skull, hair wreath and a VEERAC engine. Groups may arrange in advance for a living history program presented by interpreters in authentic costumes. Choices of programs include Tastes and Sounds of Minnesota in the Civil War, Campaigning for Lincoln, Civil War Christmas, Early Education in Anoka, Fashion Trends, and Quilts and their Stories.

Seasons/Hours: Year-round: 10 am–8 pm Tu; 10 am–5 pm W–F; 10 am–4 pm Sa; group tours by appointment

Cost: Adults: $3; youth 6–17: $2; children 5 and under and ACHS members: free

Address: 2135 3rd Ave N, Anoka, MN 55303

Phone/Fax: Ph: 763.421.0600; Fax: 763.323.0218

E-mail: achs@ac-hs.org

Website:	www.ac-hs.org
Directions:	In Anoka at the intersection of 3rd Ave and Golf St.
Don't miss this:	Guided walking tours of historical downtown Anoka can be arranged through the Anoka County Historical Society. The guides will present a then-and-now look at Anoka. A brochure is available for those who wish a self-guided tour of the city.

ARD GODFREY HOUSE

③ *Description:*

Ard Godfrey House

Ard Godfrey moved from Maine to Minnesota and opened the first sawmill in at the Falls of St. Anthony. In 1849 he built a house with the first lumber from the mill. It is this house which is now the oldest remaining building in St. Anthony, now Minneapolis. In 1905 the house was bought by the Hennepin County Territorial Pioneers and was moved to be on display for the Semi-Centennial Celebration. The house was then moved to its present location and given to the city of Minneapolis. It was operated as a museum from 1914 to 1943. The house was restored during the 1970s and was reopened to the public in 1979. The Women's Club of Minneapolis restored the building and maintains a staff for the summer public tours.

Seasons/Hours:	Memorial Day–Sept: 12 pm–3:30 pm F–Su; special tours can be arranged throughout the year
Cost:	Adults: $2, seniors and students: $1
Address:	45 Ortman St NE, Minneapolis, MN 55414
Phone:	612.379.9707
Website:	www.twincities.citysearch.com/profile/5588794
Directions:	Located along the Falls of St. Anthony on the Mississippi River. Central Ave at University SE in Richard Chute Square, between Riverplace and St. Anthony Main.

BARTHOLOMEW HOUSE

(4) Description: This house, built in the 1852 by Mrs. and General Riley Bartholomew, is the oldest house in Richfield. The Bartholomew House has been restored to its original Minnesota farmhouse style and is listed on the National Register of Historic Places. It now serves as headquarters for the Richfield Historical Society.

Hours: By appointment

Cost: Free, $1 donation suggested

Address: 6901 Lyndale Ave S, Richfield, MN 55423

Phone: 612.866.1294

Directions: Located on the east side of the Wood Lake Nature Center. It is on the corner of W 69th St and Lyndale Ave S.

BLOOMINGTON HISTORICAL MUSEUM

(5) Description: The old town hall, built in 1892, serves as the Bloomington Historical Museum. This museum features early pioneer artifacts and documents.

Seasons/Hours: Mar–Dec: 1:30 pm–4 pm Su (except holiday weekends); other times by appointment

Cost: Free, donations accepted

Address: 10206 Penn Ave S, Bloomington, MN 55431

Phone: 952.881.4327 or call city of Bloomington 952.563.8700

Website: www.bloomingtonmn.org/attractions.asp

Directions: The Historical Museum is located at Penn Ave S and Old Shakopee Rd.

BROOKLYN PARK HISTORICAL FARM

(6) Description: This restored farmhouse depicts early twentieth century rural Minnesota. There are hands on activities and living history events in the fall. The first full weekend in December is the highlight of the year, with the Old-Fashioned Farm Christmas. Come on over and have a picnic, play some games, or experience what it used to be like to do chores around the house. There's plenty for everyone to do.

Seasons/Hours:	May 1–1st weekend of Dec: group tours: mid-June–mid-Aug: 1 pm–4 pm W & Su; call for more information on special events
Cost:	Tours: $4 per person; summer: adults: $4, children 12 and under: $3
Address:	4345 101st Ave N, Brooklyn Park, MN 55443
Phone/Fax:	763.493.4604
E-mail:	bprecprog@ci.brooklyn-park.mn.us
Website:	www.ci.brooklyn-park.mn.us/government/ recreation/histfarm.html
Directions:	Hwy 252 N to 93rd Ave N, then W to Noble Pkwy., N to 101st, then E to the site.

CARVER COUNTY HISTORICAL SOCIETY

(7) *Description:*	This society is dedicated to keeping people connected to the past via local history exhibits, a veterans' exhibit and programs for schools, children and adults. The society also runs a local history and genealogy library, holding materials and records such as local newspapers, photographs and local history book.
Seasons/Hours:	Year-round: 10 am–4:30 pm M–F; 10 am–3 pm Sa
Cost:	Free
Address:	555 W 1st St, Waconia, MN 55387
Phone:	Ph: 952.442.4234
E-mail:	historical@co.carver.mn.us
Website:	www.carvercountyhistoricalsociety.org
Directions:	From Hwy 5 in Waconia, go N on Maple St S to 1st St W. Turn left and go 2½ blocks.

CHASKA HISTORICAL SOCIETY

(8) *Description:*	The Chaska Historical Society honors the rich heritage of Chaska's community. As of October 2003, the History Center is moving from their location on the second floor of the historic Klein Mansion to W 4th St. Their collections include extensive photographs, maps, scrapbooks, letters and Native American artifacts.
Seasons/Hours:	Year-round: 1 pm–5 pm W
Cost:	Free

Address:	112 W 4th St, Chaska, MN 55318
Phone:	952.448.6077
E-mail:	chaska@chaska-chamber.org
Website:	www.chaska-chamber.org
Directions:	Klein Mansion is at 4th and Walnut, across from City Square. New location is just about a block W.

 Anoka is the Halloween capital of the world.

COMO-HARRIET STREETCAR LINE

⑨ *Description:*	The streetcar line brings back the memories of when the trolley was the main source of public transportation. There had been over 500 miles of track with over 1,000 trolleys that ran throughout the Twin Cities. Today, you will be taken back in time to the days of the trolley on a 15-minute trip, starting at this reproduced 1900 station at Linden Hills and covers two miles to Lake Calhoun and back.
Seasons/Hours:	May 3–May 11: 12:30 pm–dusk Sa–Su; May 16–Sept 7: 6:30 pm–dusk M–F; 12:30 pm–dusk Sa–Su; Sept 13–Nov 30: 12:30 pm–dusk Sa–Su; check for special events and other times
Cost:	Adults: $1.50, children 3 and under: free
Address:	2330 W 42nd St (at Lake Harriet), Minneapolis, MN 55410
Phone:	651.228.0263
E-mail:	mtmuseum@hotmail.com
Website:	www.mtmuseum.org/
Directions:	The location of the line is SW of downtown Minneapolis. There are two stations available for boarding: the Linden Hills Station is at the intersection of Queen Ave S and W 42nd St. The Lake Calhoun platform is on Richfield Road, S of W 36th St.

To keep one city from outgrowing the other, both Minneapolis and St. Paul's census takers were kidnapped in the 1800s.

DAKOTA CITY HERITAGE VILLAGE

⑩ **Description:** This is a re-created turn-of-the-twentieth-century village. There is a variety of exhibits, demonstrations and programs. A living history program is available as well as educational programs for school groups May through October. The museum has exhibits including tractors and other farm equipment.

The village includes the following buildings: a depot, a fire barn, jail, cabin, schoolhouse, church, drug store, bank, general store, bandstand, post office, emporium, blacksmith shop, barbershop, harness shop, newspaper office, law office, town hall, library, photography studio, and a typical two-story house.

Call for more information about special events such as Village Christmas, Victorian Tea, Village Harvest Night and Grand History Days.

Seasons/Hours: May–Sept: 10 am–4 pm M–Sa; village open during special events and the county fair

Cost: Varies with events

Address: 4008 W 220th St, Farmington, MN 55024

Phone: 651.460.8050

E-mail: info@dakotacity.org

Website: www.dakotacity.org/index.htm

Directions: Located in Farmington on 220th St W, just W of Denmark Ave S of the main road on the corner of 2nd and 220th in the Dakota Fairgrounds.

HENNEPIN HISTORY MUSEUM

⑪ **Description:** The Hennepin County Museum offers a variety of exhibits that rotate and outstanding collections of textiles, costumes and quilts. Exhibits focus on many subjects, some of which include the following: History—Growth and Development of Minneapolis and Hennepin County; Woodlands and Prairies—Objects and Photos from the Dakota and Ojibwe. There is also an extensive library and archives holding over 100,000 items at the museum.

Seasons/Hours: 10 am–2 pm Tu; 1 pm–5 pm W; 1 pm–8 pm Th; 1 pm–3 pm F–Sa; 1 pm–5 pm Su; call to schedule a guided tour—tour themes and scheduling can be customized

Cost: Adults: $2, children and seniors: $1

Address: 2303 3rd Ave S, Minneapolis, MN 55404

Phone/Fax:	Ph: 612.870.1329; Fax: 612.870.1320
E-mail:	hhmuseum@mtn.org
Website:	www.hhmuseum.org/mu/mu.htm
Directions:	Located in the Washburn Fair Oaks Park, just W of 35W between E 22nd St and E 24th St.

HISTORIC MURPHY'S LANDING

⑫ *Description:* Historic Murphy's Landing is a living history museum on the Minnesota River. It is a reconstructed village dating from the 1840–1890 time period. There is a fur trading post, farms and an 1880 townsite. Check out the interpretive center with a gift shop. Murphy's Landing hosts a variety of special events; see website for details.

Seasons/Hours: Spring–Oct: 10 am–5 pm weekends;
Dec: 10 am–4 pm Sa–Su

Cost: Adults: $8.50; youth and seniors: $7;
park district patrons: $1 off per ticket

Address: 2187 E Hwy 101, Shakopee, MN 55379

Phone/Fax: Ph: 952.445.6900; Fax: 952.403.9489

E-mail: wwwstaff@hml.org

Website: www.threeriversparkdistrict.org/outdoor_ed/murphys_landing/index.com

Directions: Murphy's Landing is 23 mi. SW of Minneapolis. Take I-394 W until I-169 S. Then take Hwy 101 W about four mi. to the entrance of the landing, which is one mi. W of ValleyFair.

HOOPER BOWLER HILLSTROM HOUSE

⑬ *Description:* Sanford Hooper, a local businessman, built the house in 1871. The Bowlers purchased the house in 1886, and added a kitchen, a buttery, and perhaps the most unusual addition was a two-story outhouse, accessible from the second story of the house. The Hillstroms bought the house in 1900. It stayed in the family until 1975, when the Belle Plaine Historical Society purchased it. The house has been restored for three different periods: 1850s, late 1800s and early 1900s.

Seasons/Hours: Memorial Day–Labor Day: 1 pm–4 pm Su; other times by appointment

Cost: $2

Address:	410 N Cedar St, Box 73, Belle Plaine, MN 56011
Phone/Fax:	952.873.6109
Website:	www.frontiernet.net/~bellepln/Local_Attractions.htm
Directions:	From Hwy 169, N on Cedar St. The house is in northern Belle Plaine, S of Court Square, between E Court St and E State St.

JOHN H. STEVENS HOUSE MUSEUM

⑭ *Description:*	This house was finished in 1850. It was the first permanent settler's house on the west side of the Mississippi River. The house has been considered the birthplace of Minneapolis. It was originally located near the Hennepin Ave. Bridge at the current site of the Post Office. The Stevens House was moved to its present site at Minnehaha Park in 1896 through the efforts of 7,000 school children. Tours are available upon request. Walking tours of Minnehaha Park start at the Stevens House on Sundays during July and August.
Seasons/Hours:	Year-round: 1 pm–5 pm Sa–Su
Cost:	Adults: $2; youth 12–18: $1
Address:	4901 Minnehaha Ave, PO Box 17241, Minneapolis, MN 55417
Phone:	612.722.2220
Website:	www.nps.gov/miss/maps/model/side/stevens_house.html
Directions:	Located at Minnehaha Park across from the Minnehaha Depot.

TRIVIA In 1880 the University of Minnesota was the first in the nation to hire a woman as a full professor.

MILL CITY MUSEUM

⑮ *Description:*	Come take a tour through the eight-story Flour Tower. Experience and learn about the industry that helped build Minneapolis to be the city it is today. With hands-on exhibits and many displays, you will learn the story of Minneapolis' flour industry and the effect it had on the world.
Seasons/Hours:	Year-round: 10 am–5 pm Tu–Sa; 12 pm–5 pm Su; 10 am–9 pm 1st Th of each month; Memorial Day–Labor Day: 10 am–5 pm M; call for holiday hours

Cost:	Adults: $7, seniors: $5, college students: $5, students: $4, children 3 and under: free, MHS members: free, groups 10 or more: $6
Address:	704 S 2nd St, Minneapolis, MN 55401
Phone:	612.341.7555
E-mail:	mcm@mnhs.org
Website:	www.millcitymuseum.org/about/
Directions:	Located N of the Hubert H. Humphrey Metrodome. It is on the corner of 11th Ave and 2nd St on the west bank of the Mississippi River.

TRIVIA

Wheaties, otherwise known as "The Breakfast of Champions," was created by accident in 1921, when a Minneapolis clinician who was mixing bran gruel for his patients splashed some on the stove. He brought it to what is now General Mills, and shortly thereafter a contest was held to name the product.

MINNEHAHA DEPOT

Minnesota Historical Society

Minnehaha Depot

⑯ *Description:*	This is a restored 1875 Milwaukee Road Depot. It is located in the midst of Minnehaha Park. The depot has exhibits of railroad memorabilia and general information on the railroad. Volunteers may be doing demonstrations. This site is managed by the Minnesota Transportation Museum.
Seasons/Hours:	Memorial Day–Labor Day: 12:30 pm–4:30 pm Su & holidays; other times by appointment
Cost:	Free
Address:	PO Box 17240, Nokomis Station, Minneapolis, MN 55417

Phone:	651.228.0263
E-mail:	minnehahadepot@mnhs.org
Website:	www.mnhs.org/places/sites/md/
Directions:	3½ blocks N of Hwy 62 on 26th Ave.

MINNETONKA HISTORICAL SOCIETY

⑰ *Description:* Come and visit this beautiful Victorian home of Charles H. Burwell. Burwell was the manager of Minnetonka Mills Company until 1886 when it closed because of the competition of mills in Minneapolis. He remained successful and built a home in Minnetonka for his wife and children. The restored house, as well as the pictures, artifacts and letters will give you a peek into what life in the 1880s was like.

Seasons/Hours: By appointment; watch for special events

Cost: Free; group rates

Address: 13209 McGinty Rd E, Minnetonka, MN 55343

Phone/Fax: Ph: 952.939.8219; Fax: 952.939.8244

E-mail: lronbeck@eminnetonka.com

Website: www.minnetonka-history.org

Directions: Located in the Burwell Park just N of Minnetonka Blvd in between Cedar Lake Rd and Chase Dr.

The first Tonka truck was built in 1947 in Mound. Tonka means "great" in Dakota and was named after Lake Minnetonka which means "great water."

NEW BRIGHTON AREA HISTORY CENTER

⑱ *Description:* This is an 1887 Soo Line Depot that has been renovated and furnished with railroad memorabilia and area historical pictures and items. See a 1945 Great Northern caboose and railroad work cart, luggage cart and mail cart.

Seasons/Hours: June–Sept: 1 pm–4 pm Sa & Su; or by appointment; call or check website for special events

Cost: Free

Address:	Long Lake Regional Park, 1500 Old Hwy 8, New Brighton, MN 55112
Mail to:	PO Box 120624, New Brighton, MN 55112
Phone:	Ph: 651.633.4701
Website:	www.exploreminnesota.com, search for "New Brighton Area History Center"
Directions:	From I-35W, take the Hwy 96 Exit, turn W to Hwy 8 (T-intersection), turn S (left) and follow signs to Long Lake Regional Park. The History Center is about ½ mi. into the park.

OUR LADY OF LOURDES CHURCH

(19) Description: This is the oldest continuously used church in Minneapolis. It is near the Falls of St. Anthony where Father Hennepin first saw the Falls. The church is a US historic landmark.

Our Lady of Lourdes Church

Hours: 9 am–5 pm M–F; 9 am–12 pm Sa

Cost: Donation for guided tours

Address: 1 Lourdes Place, Minneapolis, MN 55414

Phone/Fax: Ph: 612.379.2259; Fax: 612.379.2259

E-mail: lourdes@usinternet.com

Website: www.ourladyoflourdes.com

Directions: Located on the east side of the Mississippi River on E Hennepin Ave above Riverplace.

PLYMOUTH HISTORICAL SOCIETY

(20) Description: The collections of the Plymouth Historical Society are housed in the old Town Hall, which was built in 1859. Displays focus on Plymouth's early history and include plat maps, clothing, school memorabilia, artifacts and photos.

Seasons/Hours: Year-round: 1 pm–4 pm 3rd Su of month; 7 pm–9 pm 4th M of month; or by appointment

Cost:	Donations
Address:	Old Town Hall, 3605 Fernbrook Ln., Plymouth, MN 55447
Phone:	763.559.9201; City of Plymouth: 763.509.5000
Website:	www.rootsweb.com/~mnhennep/society.htm; City of Plymouth: www2.ci.plymouth.mn.us
Directions:	Located not far from the City Center in Plymouth Creek Park.

SCOTT COUNTY HISTORICAL SOCIETY

㉑ *Description:*	The Scott County Historical Society maintains the Stans Museum and the Stans House, home of Maurice Stans, who served under President Nixon as Secretary of Commerce. This restored 1908 Dutch colonial bungalow reflects life in the early 1900s. The museum also displays artifacts that share the stories of Scott County's people and places. Its genealogy library holds a collection of microfilm, books, maps and photographs.
Hours:	9 am–4 pm Tu, W, F; 9 am–8 pm Th; 10 am–3 pm Sa
Cost:	Adults: $2, students: $1; members and children under 5: free
Address:	235 S Fuller St, Shakopee, MN 55379
Phone/Fax:	Ph: 952.445.0378; Fax: 952.445.4154
E-mail:	info@scottcountyhistory.org
Website:	www.scottcountyhistory.org
Directions:	Located S of the Minnesota River on Fuller St between 2nd Ave and 3rd Ave W.

UPPER ST. ANTHONY FALLS LOCK AND DAM

㉒ *Description:*	Take a look at the uppermost lock of the 29 locks on the Mississippi River. The visitor center has an observation deck or you can observe from the Stone Arch Bridge. This view will show you what power the Falls of St. Anthony have. They were once the only source of electricity for the flour and lumber milling industries in Minneapolis. Now the lock is used daily by commercial as well as leisure boats.
Seasons/Hours:	Apr–Nov: 9 am–10 pm daily
Cost:	Free
Address:	1 Portland Ave, Minneapolis, MN 55401
Phone:	612.333.5336

E-mail:	info@wildernessinquiry.org
Website:	www.mvp.usace.army.mil/recreation/default.asp?pageid= 145&subpageid=144
Directions:	Located N of the Minneapolis City Center. It is W of 35W and E of Central Ave. Take the bridge on the south side of the Mississippi River.

WELLS FARGO HISTORY MUSEUM

㉓ *Description:*	This downtown museum has an authentic stagecoach from 1863, banking tools from the turn of the century and interactive displays, including a telegraph. Also, kids and adults alike can take a ride in the reproduction stagecoach to experience the motion of early travel. Free educational tours available for school groups. Please call for reservations.
Seasons/Hours:	Year-round: 9 am–5 pm M–F
Cost:	Free
Address:	6th St and Marquette St, Skyway Level, Wells Fargo Center, Minneapolis, 55479
Phone/Fax:	Ph: 612.667.4210; Fax: 612.316.4361
Website:	www.wellsfargohistory.com/museums/mnmuseum.html
Directions:	Located on the east side of the City Center Shopping Center on the corner of 6th St and Marquette St.

WESTERN HENNEPIN COUNTY PIONEERS ASSOCIATION

㉔ *Directions:*	The museum is located in an old brick schoolhouse. There are four classrooms each with a different theme that reflect the history of the area. There is also a picture gallery. There are archives of 1,000 families with roots in western Hennepin County. Check out the carriage house and the log cabin school.
Seasons/Hours:	10 am–4 pm Sa; 10 am–1 pm research
Cost:	Free but donations appreciated
Address:	1953 W Wayzata Blvd, PO Box 332, Long Lake, MN 55356
Phone/Fax:	For tours call: 952.473.5671; Fax: 952.473.6557
Directions:	Located W of Minneapolis off Hwy 12 on Wayzata Blvd.

AFTON
HISTORICAL MUSEUM

 Description: The Afton Museum is located in the former Congregational Church building (1868) in the historic village of Afton. This restored building has a turn-of-the-century kitchen and school-room, library, military artifacts, telephone switchboard as well as an extensive photograph gallery of early schools and classes, early settlers and historic events. The lower floor of the museum has displays of early agriculture.

Find extensive files of information on area families, photographs, census records, and Afton's seven cemeteries, including a Civil War cemetery.

Seasons/Hours: Year-round: 1 pm–8 pm W; May–Oct: 1 pm–4 pm Su; call for special village events throughout the year

Cost: Free

Address: 3165 St. Croix Trl S, PO Box 178, Afton, MN 55001

Phone: 651.436.3500

E-mail: scriv@pressenter.com

Website: www.pressenter.com/~aftnhist

Directions: From I-94, go S on Cty Rd 18, which is St. Croix Trl through Afton. As Cty Rd 18 turns W, continue going S one block on St. Croix Trl. The museum is a large yellow building on the east side of the road.

ALEXANDER RAMSEY
HOUSE

 Description: One of the best preserved Victorian houses in the country, this was the home of Alexander Ramsey, Minnesota's first territorial governor. Catch a glimpse of family life beginning in the 1870s as you hear about life of three generations of the Ramsey family and their servants.

Seasons/Hours: Year-round: F–Sa 10 am–3 pm; call for group tour reservations and for special holiday hours

Cost: Adults: $8, seniors: $7, children ages 6–12: $4; children ages 5 & under and MHS members: free

Address: 265 S Exchange St, St. Paul, MN 55102

Phone: 651.296.8760 or 651.296.0100

E-mail: ramseyhouse@mnhs.org

Website: www.mnhs.org/places/sites/arh/

Directions:	The Alexander Ramsey house is located at the corner of Ramsey St, one block S of W 7th St in St. Paul.

Minnesota Historical Society

Alexander Ramsey House

GAMMELGARDEN MUSEUM

㉗ *Description:* Gammelgarden (old small farm) Museum preserves, presents and promotes Swedish immigrant heritage and history. The 11-acre museum site includes 1868 Prast Hus that was used as the first parsonage for the Elim Congregation, the 1856 Gammelkyrkan the first sanctuary of Elim Lutheran Church, the 1879 Ladugard (barn), Immigrant Hus and Swedish Stuga. A gift shop, playground and park complete the site. This is also a research site for the author of American Girl *Kirsten* stories.

Seasons/Hours: Tour schedule: May–mid-Oct: 1 pm, 2 pm & 3 pm F–Su; gift shop: May–mid-Dec: 10 am–4 pm M–Sa; 1 pm–4 pm Su; call for special events and tours

Cost: Adults: $4, children 11 and under: free

Address: 20880 Olinda Trl, Scandia, MN 55073

Mail to: 9885 202 St N, Forest Lake, MN 55025

Phone: 651.433.5053 or 651.433.3430 evenings

E-mail: lmoratzk@luthersem.edu

Website: www.scandiamn.com

Directions: From Hwy 61, go E on Hwy 97 to Cty Rd 4 and go S to Scandia.

GIBBS MUSEUM OF PIONEER AND DAKOTAH LIFE

28 Description: Costumed guides tell the story of the Gibbs family and their relationship to the Dakotah Indians. The tour goes through the farmhouse, one-room schoolhouse, sodhouse, barns, gardens, tipi and a bark lodge.

Seasons/Hours: T–F 10 am–4 pm; Su 12 pm–4 pm; closed mid-Nov–mid-April

Cost: Adults: $5; seniors: $4; children ages 2–16: $3

Address: 2097 W Larpenteur Ave, St. Paul, MN 55113

Phone: 651.646.8629

E-mail: info@rchs.com

Website: www.rchs.com

Directions: Located at the intersection of Cleveland Ave and Larpenteur Ave in St. Paul

GOVERNOR'S MANSION

29 Description: The building that is now the governor's residence was built in 1912 for Horace Hills Irvine, a St. Paul lumberman. The Irvine family lived in the house until 1965, when the mansion was donated by the family to the state. It was placed on the National Register of Historic Places in 1974. The governor's mansion is English Tudor style with 20 rooms and nine fireplaces.

Seasons/Hours: Tours by appointment

Cost: Free; photo ID required for admittance

Phone: 651.297.8177 for tours (reservations needed)

Address: 1006 Summit Ave, St. Paul, MN 55105

Website: www.admin.state.mn.us/buildings/residence/history.html

Directions: Located on historic Summit Avenue in St. Paul.

HAY LAKE SCHOOL

30 Description: This 1896 brick building, listed on the National Register of Historic Places, was the second structure of Minnesota School District #2, which was organized in 1855. Guided tours of the school and other attractions on site tell the story of the Swedish immigrants that came to live in the area. The Hay Lake School is managed by the Washington County Historical Society.

Seasons/Hours:	May–Oct: 1:30 pm–4:30 pm Sa–Su; or by appointment
Cost:	Nominal fee
Address:	Scandia, MN 55073
Write to:	Washington County Historical Society, PO Box 167, Stillwater, MN 55082
Phone:	651.433.4014
Website:	www.wchsmn.org/wchsmuseums.html
Directions:	From Scandia's Historic Corner, go one mi. S, then E of the Olinda Trl N (Cty Rd 3) and Old Marine Trl intersection.

HISTORIC FORT SNELLING

31 *Description:* This restored stone fortress opens its gates to welcome you to frontier life. Imagine that the year is 1827, and as costumed guides greet you, that you've just arrived via steamboat up the Mississippi River. Enjoy the

Historic Fort Snelling

Minnesota Historical Society

sites and sounds of the past at Historic Fort Snelling.

Seasons/Hours:	May: Sa 10 am–5 pm; Su 12 pm–5 pm; Memorial Day–Labor Day: guided tours: M–Tu 10 am–5 pm; Living History: W–Sa 10 am–5 pm; Su 12–5 pm; Sept–Oct: Sa 10 am–5 pm; Su 12 pm–5 pm; Nov–April: reservations required during school tour season
Cost:	Adults: $8, seniors: $7, children ages 6–12: $4; children ages 6 & under and MHS members: free
Address:	Fort Snelling History Center, St. Paul, MN 55111
Phone:	612.726.1171
E-mail:	ftsnelling@mnhs.org
Website:	www.mnhs.org/places/sites/hfs/index.html
Directions:	Located in St. Paul at the intersection of Hwy 5 and Hwy 55, one mi. E of the Twin Cities International Airport.

㉜ Description: This magnificent mansion built of rugged stone to great scale yet intricate detail recalls the powerful presence of James J. Hill, builder of the Great Northern Railway. Once the largest private residence in the state, the 36,000 square foot Hill House hosts dramatic programming throughout the year, including Victorian Ghost Stories, gaslight tours and lectures.

Seasons/Hours: Year-round: W–Sa 10 am–3:30 pm; Su 1 pm–3:30 pm; guided tours every 30 minutes. Call for reservations.

Cost: Adults: $8, seniors: $7, children 6–12: $4; children under 6 and MHS members: free

Address: 240 Summit Ave, St. Paul, MN 55102

Phone: 651.297.2555 or 888.727.8386

E-mail: hillhouse@mnhs.org

Website: www.mnhs.org/hillhouse

Directions: The Hill House is ½ block W of the Cathedral of St. Paul, close to the intersection of I-94 and 35E.

Don't miss this: The Minnesota Historical Society offers a guided walking tour along the marvelous Summit Ave estates May–Sept. Contact MHS for more information.

Minnesota Historical Society

James J. Hill House

JOHANNES ERICKSON LOG HOUSE MUSEUM

Description: This is a two-story log house built by Johannes Erickson in 1868. It is listed on the National Register of Historic Places.

Seasons/Hours: May–Oct: 1:30 pm–4:30 pm Sa–Su; or by appointment

Cost: Nominal fee

Address: Scandia, MN 55073

Phone: 651.433.4014

Website: www.wchsmn.org/wchsmuseums.html

Directions: From Scandia's Historic Corner, go one mi. S, then E of the Olinda Trl N (Cty Rd 3) and Old Marine Trl intersection.

LANDMARK CENTER

㉞ *Description:* In 1970 the Landmark Center, formerly the Federal Courts Building located in downtown St. Paul, was scheduled for demolition. Through the efforts of determined citizens the building was salvaged and declared a National Historic Monument. The building was then successfully restored and has been honored with numerous awards, including a top national award from the American Institute of Architects in 1980. Landmark Center's four beautiful courtrooms housed St. Paul's famous "gangster trials" during the 1930s. Landmark Center is not only known for its architectural brilliance but also its cultural events. "Sundays at Landmark" feature monthly events that educate the public on various cultures and are free or low cost.

Landmark Center

Seasons/Hours: Year-round: 8 am–5 pm M, Tu, W & F; 8 am–8 pm Th; 10 am–5 pm Sa; 12 pm–5 pm Su

Cost: Free

Address: 75 W 5th St, St. Paul, MN 55102

Phone:	651.292.3225
E-mail:	admin@landmarkcenter.org
Website:	www.landmarkcenter.org
Directions:	Landmark Center is located downtown St. Paul, across from Rice Park, the Ordway Center for the Performing Arts and the Public Library. From I-94E, exit at 5th St. From I-94W, exit at 6th St. From I-35E N, exit at Kellogg Blvd. From I-35E S, exit at Wacouta to 6th St.

MINNESOTA HISTORY CENTER

㉟ *Description:*	With its breathtaking views of downtown St. Paul and the State Capitol, the Minnesota Historical Society History Center is an architectural masterpiece made of Minnesota materials, from Rockville granite to Winona limestone. A great place for a family outing offering something for everyone, it is an innovative museum and a modern library.
Seasons/Hours:	Year-round: 10 am–8 pm Tu; 10 am–3 pm W–F; 10 am–5 pm Sa; 12 pm–5 pm Su; call for holiday hours
Cost:	Free
Address:	345 Kellogg Blvd W, St. Paul, MN 55102
Phone:	651.296.6126 or 800.657.3773; group reservations: 651.297.7258
E-mail:	webmaster@mnhs.org
Website:	www.mnhs.org/places/historycenter
Directions:	Located at the intersection of I-35E and I-94, on the western edge of downtown St. Paul, on the corner of Kellogg Blvd and John Ireland Blvd.

MINNESOTA STATE CAPITOL HISTORIC SITE

㊱ *Description:*	Original furnishings and vivid colors of the restored Senate, House, Supreme Court and Rathskellar Cafe bring to life this working masterpiece by acclaimed architect Cass Gilbert. See the legislature in action in the historic House and Senate chambers. Free guided tours begin on the hour until one hour before closing. Weather permitting, tour groups can visit the *Quadriga*, or golden horses that loom high atop the building. Special events, tours and educational programs are available for modest fees throughout the year.
Seasons/Hours:	Year-round: 9 am–4 pm M–F; 10 am–3pm Sa;

	1 pm–4 pm Su; closed holidays (except Presidents Day)
Cost:	Educational groups: $2–$4; adult groups and upcoming events: $7, $6, $4; members: $5; public tours: free
Address:	Capitol Historic Site, Minnesota State Capitol, Room B-59, 75 Rev. Martin Luther King Jr. Blvd, St. Paul, MN 55155
Phone:	651.296.2881
E-mail:	statecapitol@mnhs.org
Website:	www.mnhs.org/places/sites/msc
Directions:	Located in St. Paul N of downtown, accessible from I-94 and 35E.

Minnesota Historical Society

Minnesota State Capitol Historic Site

MINNESOTA TRANSPORTATION MUSEUM

㊲ *Description:*	The Minnesota Transportation Museum was originally organized to save a single streetcar. Since that time, the MTM has grown to include five operating sites including the Osceola and St. Croix Valley Railway and the Como-Harriet Streetcar Line. It also encompasses numerous depots and museums at a number of different locations, spanning means of transportation from old fashioned buses and streetcars to steamboats. The Jackson Street Roundhouse is a good place to start; it houses displays, archives and an audio-visual theater. Group tours are available by appointment.
Seasons/Hours:	Year-round: W 10 am–4 pm; Sa 10 am–5 pm; group tours by appointment; closed holiday weekends
Cost:	$5
Address:	193 Pennsylvania Ave E, St. Paul, MN 55101

Phone:	651.228.0263
E-mail:	mtmuseum@hotmail.com
Website:	www.mtmuseum.org
Directions:	The Jackson Street Roundhouse is N of the State Capitol. Take the Pennsylvania Ave. Exit off of 35E and go W two blocks.

NORTH ST. PAUL HISTORICAL SOCIETY

㊳ Description: Platted in 1887, North St. Paul was one of Minnesota's first planned communities. Before a single lot was purchased, the entire town was platted to include places for homes, businesses, churches and schools. The North St. Paul Historical Society offers a walking tour brochure of the North St. Paul neighborhood as well as a museum. The entire walking tour is about a mile and a half long and takes you past 23 sites including churches, civic buildings and houses in the historical downtown area. The museum houses items from North St. Paul's past, such as furniture, a piano and an organ, all made in North St. Paul. School memorabilia and photos are also on display.

Seasons/Hours: Year-round: F 1 pm–4 pm; Sa 10 am–1 pm; tours by appointment

Cost: Free

Address: 2666 E 7th Ave, North St. Paul, MN 55109

Phone: 651.779.6402

Directions: From St. Paul, take Hwy 36 E toward Stillwater. Turn right on Margaret St. by the 40-foot-tall cement snowman. Go approximately two blocks and turn left onto 7th.

SIBLEY HOUSE HISTORICAL SITE

㊴ Description: This was the home of Henry Sibley, the first governor of Minnesota. He came to this area with the American Fur Company. This historic site includes four limestone buildings, which were

Sibley House Historical Site

part of the early settlements of the Minnesota. The buildings have been furnished with mid-nineteenth century interiors and exhibits. The restored historic structures include a fur company cold store and the Jean Baptiste Faribault Hotel.

Seasons/Hours: May–Oct: 10 pm–3:30 pm Th–M; tours are given of the site with the last starting at 3:45 pm

Cost: Adults: $5, senior citizens: $4, children 6–12: $2; MHS members: free

Address: 1357 Sibley Memorial Hwy, Mendota, MN 55150

Phone: 651.452.1596

E-mail: sibleyhouse@mnhs.org

Website: www.mnhs.org/places/sites/shs

Directions: Located on Sibley Memorial Hwy (Hwy 13) in Mendota just to the NE of the Mendota Bridge, between Hwy 55 and I-35 E on Main St in Mendota.

STONE HOUSE MUSEUM

 Description: This old 1872 township hall houses period clothing, household items and a Swedish kitchen, depicting life for the early settlers in the area. Commercial saw equipment, also on display, was used in some of the first sawmills in the state—one built at Marine on St. Croix and another in Stillwater.

Seasons/Hours: July 4–Labor Day: Sa & Su 2 pm–5 pm; or by appointment

Cost: Free, donations appreciated

Address: Oak St and 5th St, Marine on St. Croix, MN 55047

Phone: 651.433.2061

Directions: Located in Marine on St. Croix at the intersection of Oak St and 5th St.

WARDEN'S HOUSE MUSEUM

④① *Description:* This 14-room stone house was built in 1853 to house the wardens of the Minnesota Territorial and State Prison. It is one of the oldest residences still standing in the state and is on the National Register of Historic Places. Today it has artifacts representing the history of the county.

Seasons/Hours: May–Oct: Th–Sa 1 pm–5 pm

Cost: Adults: $3; youth under 17: $1

Address:	602 N Main St, PO Box 167, Stillwater, MN 55082
Phone:	651.439.5956
E-mail:	information@wchsmn.org
Website:	www.wchsmn.org
Directions:	From I-94, take Hwy 95 N into Stillwater, where it turns into Main St Follow this street downtown, and the Warden's House will be on your left, across the street from the Minnesota Zephyr Train Station parking lot.

WOODBURY HERITAGE HOUSE AND GARDEN

㊷ *Description:*	The building now known as the Heritage House was built around 1870 as an attachment to a log cabin. The garden has local heirloom plants that have been donated by members and friends of the society. A butterfly garden provides a naturalized look, and trees have been planted as memorials to past residents. The Woodbury Heritage Society also maintains the Family/City History Research Room.
Seasons/Hours:	June–Sept: 1 pm–4 pm, 2nd & 4th Su of the month
Cost:	Free
Address:	8301 Valley Creek Rd., Woodbury, MN 55125
Phone:	651.714.3564
Directions:	From 694, exit at Lake Rd and go E to Radio Dr. From I-94, exit at Radio Dr and go S to Lake Rd Garden is at the intersection of Radio Dr and Lake Rd.

METRO AREA MINNESOTA FESTIVALS

LISTED ALPHABETICALLY

ANNUAL GREAT SCARECROW FESTIVAL

Description: If you're in the mood for autumn festivities, come to Belle Plaine and see over 100 of Emma Krumbee's unique, handcrafted scarecrows. This intriguing display of scarecrows is one you'll want to browse through again and again. This is a hot spot for good country fun for the whole family. There are pony and camel rides, wagon rides, games, music, and lots of food.

Occurrence: Late September–early October. Activities running from 10 am–6 pm

Cost: $3.50, children under 3: free

Phone: 952.873.3006

Website: www.emmakrumbees.com/scarecrow.html

Directions: Located 45 min. S of Minneapolis and 45 min. N of Mankato on Hwy 169. Follow the billboards.

JULIFEST

Description: This July festival features food, music and dancing. Activities include games for all ages, bake and craft sales, bingo, raffles, a polka mass and street dance.

Occurrence: July

Phone/Fax: Ph: 952.445.1979; Fax: 952.445.8351

E-mail: Kmphilipp@aol.com

Directions: St. Mark's Church hosts Julifest; it is located at 3rd Avenue and Atwood Street in Shakopee.

LITTLE LOG HOUSE
ANTIQUE POWER SHOW

Description:	This village is a representation of a pioneer town. Starting with the little log cabin found by Steve and Sylvia Bauer, the village has now grown to include 45 buildings, including a butcher shop, general store, saloon, blacksmith shop, post office and church. Come see the sights and enjoy parades, threshing shows, a beautiful garden, good food and more.
Occurrence:	July, 8 am–5 pm daily; pancake breakfast 7 am daily
Cost:	Day passes: adults: $8; weekend passes: $15; children 12 and under: free
Write to:	13746 220th St E, Hastings, MN 55033
Phone/Fax:	Ph: 651.437.2693; Fax: 651.437.6394
E-mail:	info@littleloghouseshow.com
Website:	www.littleloghouseshow.com/llhantiqueshow.html
Directions:	Six mi. S of Hastings on Hwy 61, E one mi. on 220th St.

NOWTHEN
THRESHING SHOW

Description:	Enjoy day-to-day activities and implements of 1890 to 1920. Watch threshing and plowing or visit the sawmill, lathe mill or shingle mill. Tractors, engines and antique vehicles are on display. Activities include a children's barnyard, train rides, flea market, daily parade and tractor pulls. Craft and activities building features spinning, quilting, weaving, pottery and other handicrafts.
Occurrence:	Third weekend in August
Cost:	Day passes: adults: $6; family: $12; 3-day passes: adults: $12; families: $24; children under 12: free
Write to:	7415 Old Viking Blvd NW, Nowthen, MN 55303
Phone:	763.295.2600
E-mail:	nhpamn@yahoo.com
Website:	www.nowthenthreshing.com
Directions:	6 mi. NE of Elk River on Old Viking Blvd NW, W of Hwy 169. Watch for signs.

 **RIVERTOWN DAYS**

Description:	This city-wide festival is one event you won't want to miss. See the music festival, games, parade, carnival, high-action bike shows, lumberjack shows, flea market, arts and crafts fair, fireworks display and much more.
Occurrence:	Third full weekend in July
Write to:	111 E 3rd St, Hastings, MN 55033
Phone/Fax:	Ph: 651.437.6775; Fax: 651.437.2697
E-mail:	info@hastingsmn.org
Website:	www.hastingsmn.org
Directions:	Events take place throughout Hastings. From I-94, take Hwy 61 S, or from I-94 take Hwy 52 S to Hwy 55 E. Both will take you right through Hastings.

 **STILLWATER LUMBERJACK DAYS**

Description:	This is Stillwater's annual celebration on the beautiful St. Croix River. Come to Lowell Park for concerts, lumberjack shows and fireworks. Other activities include a treasure hunt, parade, old-style baseball games and the Minnesota State Strongman competition.
Occurrence:	Mid-July
Cost:	Free
Write to:	L.D. Festival Association, Inc., PO Box 21, Stillwater, MN 55082
Phone:	651.430.2306
E-mail:	info@lumberjackdays.com
Website:	www.lumberjackdays.com
Directions:	Stillwater is ½ hour E of Minneapolis/St. Paul on Hwy 36. Turn left (N) on Manning Ave, then right (E) on Hwy 96 and right (S) on Hwy 95, which runs right through Stillwater.

COUNTIES INCLUDED IN THIS SECTION:

ANOKA COUNTY was established in 1857. It was named for the Dakota word meaning "on both sides," referring to its location on the Rum River. The county seat is Anoka. The area is 446 square miles, which ranks 76th in the state. Population is 298,084 people, which ranks 4th in Minnesota. Population density 703 people per square mile, which ranks 3rd in the state.

DAKOTA COUNTY was established in 1849. It was named for the Dakota people. "Dakota" means an alliance or league. The county seat is Hastings. The area is 586 square miles, which ranks 57th in the state. Population is 355,904 people, which ranks 3rd Minnesota. Population density is 625 people per square mile, which ranks 4th in the state.

HENNEPIN COUNTY was established in 1852. It was named for Father Louis Hennepin who explored the upper Mississippi River. The county seat is Minneapolis. The area is 606 square miles, which ranks 54th in the state. Population is 1,116,200 people, which ranks highest in Minnesota. Population density is 2,005 people per square mile, which ranks 2nd in the state.

RAMSEY COUNTY was established in 1849. It was named after the first governor of the Minnesota Territory, Alexander Ramsey. The county seat is St. Paul. The area is 170 square miles, which ranks 87th in the state. The population is 511,035 people, which ranks 2nd in Minnesota. Population density is 3280.6 people per square mile, which ranks 1st in the state.

SCOTT COUNTY was established in 1853. It was named for General Winfield Scott, who ran for the presidency in 1852 and served during the War of 1812 and the Mexican War. The county seat is Shakopee. The area is 369 square miles, which ranks 86th in the state. Population is 89,498 people, which ranks 10th in Minnesota. Population density is 250.9 people per square mile, which ranks 6th in the state.

WASHINGTON COUNTY was established in 1849. It was named after the first US president George Washington. The county seat is Stillwater. The area is 423 square miles, which ranks 83rd in the state. The population is 201,130 people, which ranks 5th in Minnesota. Population density is 513.5 people per square mile, which ranks 5th in the state.

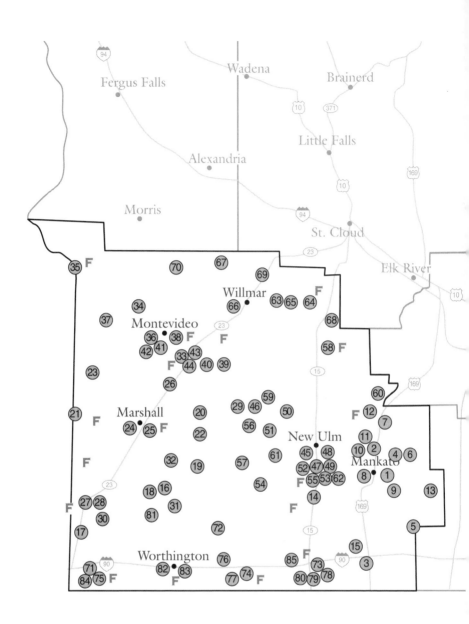

SOUTHWEST MINNESOTA

ATTRACTIONS WITHIN AN HOUR'S DRIVE OF:

(#) = historic sites   F = festivals

Listings in grey print are found in other sections but are within an hour's drive of the city.

BLUE EARTH COUNTY HISTORICAL SOCIETY

① *Description:* The Heritage Center includes an exhibit gallery holding displays of Native American, early pioneer and twentieth century items. Special exhibits include one of local author Maud Hart Lovelace who wrote the Betsy-Tacy series, a diorama of Mankato from the 1800s plus regularly changing displays of artifacts. Also on-site is a museum store providing archival supplies, souvenirs and books, and the research center library providing microfilmed newspapers, photographs and books.

Seasons/Hours: Year-round: 10 am–12 pm & 1 pm–4 pm T–Sa

Cost: Adults: $2, students: $1; children under 5 and members: free; daily access to research center: $3

Address: 415 E Cherry St, Mankato, MN 56001

Phone: 507.345.5566

E-mail: bechs@juno.com; bechs-research@juno.com (for research)

Website: www.rootsweb.com/~mnbechs

Directions: From Hwy 169, take the Mankato/N Mankato Exit and turn left. Go to 4th St, turn left to 5th St and turn right. Go approx. three blocks to the stop sign at Cherry St, take a right, then immediately left into the alley to the parking lot.

E. ST. JULIEN COX HOUSE

② *Description:* This fabulous example of Gothic/Italianate architecture was built in 1871 and is listed on the National Register of Historic Places. Learn about Cox, the first mayor of St. Peter, a state legislator, senator and district judge. Tour the restored house with a costumed guide who will conduct an interpretive tour of the house and grounds. Visit in the spring and summer to participate in a lawn party and view the extraordinary garden, or during the holiday season for "Christmas at the Cox House," which occurs the first two weekends in December.

Seasons/Hours: May and early Sept: 10 am–4 pm Th, F & Sa

Cost: Adults: $3, children 12 and under: free

Address: 500 N Washington Ave, St. Peter, MN 56082

Write to: Nicollet County Historical Society, 1851 Minnesota Ave, St. Peter, MN 56082

Phone: 507.934.4309 or 507.934.2160

E-mail: spcham6@mnic.net

Directions:	From Hwy 169 in St. Peter, turn W on Skaro St. and go about six blocks to the intersection of Skaro and Hwy 22.

ETTA ROSS HISTORICAL MUSEUM

③ *Description:*	Explore the Etta Ross Historical Museum, which includes the 1867 Wakefield House and the Good Shepherd Episcopal Church. Take a glance into the past at the outdoor exhibits available during the summer which include the Woodland School, Krosch log house, a blacksmith shop and a post office.
Seasons/Hours:	Year-round: 2 pm–5 pm Tu–Sa; or by appointment
Cost:	Free
Address:	405 6th St, Blue Earth, MN 56013
Phone:	507.526.5421
Directions:	Take Hwy 169 to Blue Earth, then go W on 6th St.

GELDER SAWMILL

④ *Description:*	Visit the last remaining steam-powered sawmill in Minnesota. Don't miss the sawing demonstrations performed on the second Sunday of each summer month.
Seasons/Hours:	Year-round: 1 pm–4 pm Su
Cost:	Free
Address:	PO Box 240, Elysian, MN 56028
Phone:	507.267.4620 507.357.4319
E-mail:	museum@lchs.mus.mn.us
Website:	www.lchs.mus.mn.us/county/geldner.html
Directions:	From St. Peter, take Cty Rd 99 to Cleveland, then go S (right) on Hwy 15. It will go by Beaver Dam along the lake, and the sawmill is on the right side. Watch for signs.

KREMER HOUSE LIBRARY AND MUSEUM

⑤ *Description:*	The Minnesota Lake Historical Society and the Minnesota Lake Friends of the Library have preserved this beautiful 1902 brick mansion and partially refurbished it to reflect the era. The museum houses a replica of the Shostag Mill, area memorabilia,

photographs, original china and the Minnesota Lake Centennial Quilt. Other exhibits change every few months, with different themes from animals and household implements to crafts and early Minnesota Lake. One of the Library and Museum's major draws is the family history and genealogy.

Seasons/Hours: Museum hours: 12:40 pm–4:30 pm M; 8 am–4:30 pm Tu–W; or by appointment; library hours: 2 pm–5 pm Tu

Cost: Free

Address: 317 Main St, Minnesota Lake, MN 56068

Phone: 507.462.3420

E-mail: mlfamily@bevcomm.net

Website: www.minnesotalake.com/attractions1.htm

Directions: Minnesota Lake's downtown only has two blocks! The Kremer House Library and Museum is the big brick mansion.

LE SUEUR COUNTY HISTORICAL SOCIETY MUSEUM

(6) *Description:* Ranked as one of the ten best museums in Minnesota, this 1895 brick schoolhouse is not to be missed. Perhaps most impressive is the 10,000-year-old prehistoric bison skull on display; it is one of the most complete skulls ever found in Minnesota. Other noteworthy displays inlcude a late nineteenth century general store and living quarters, the church room with donations from nine different Catholic churches, and the art room, with works from well-known artists, including silhouettes by local artist Earle Swain.

Seasons/Hours: June–Aug: 1 pm–5 pm W–Su; May and Sept: 1 pm–5 pm Sa–Su; closed Memorial Day and Labor Day

Cost: Free

Address: 301 NE 2nd St, Elysian, MN 56028

Phone: 507.267.4620

E-mail: museum@lchs.lmas.mn.us

Website: www.lchs.mus.mn.us/museum/index.html

Directions: Near the water tower on the highest hill in Elysian.

TRIVIA

Le Center is home to the Jolly Green Giant who first appeared in 1928 promoting the peas of the valley. He was so popular that Minnesota Valley Canning Company changed its name to the Green Giant Company.

LE SUEUR MUSEUM

⑦ **Description:** A converted school building is home to the Le Sueur Museum, featuring a complete history of the world-famous Green Giant Company. It also has excellent displays of veterinary medicine and an "old time" drug store. Other exhibits include the Radio Room, Early Schools and Hotels, Agriculture in the Valley and Military Display. The research center includes microfilmed records of Le Sueur newspapers from the late 1800s as well as other helpful resources.

Seasons/Hours: Year-round: Tu–Th 10 am–4:30 pm; Memorial Day–Labor Day: Tu–Th 10 am–4:30 pm, F–Sa 1 pm–4:30 pm

Cost: Free, donations appreciated

Address: 709 N 2nd St, Le Sueur, MN 56058

Phone: 507.665.2050

Website: www.lesueurchamber.org/about_lesueur/visiting.php#history

Directions: Follow Main St to Elm St Go E on Elm St for one block to 2nd St.

MINNEOPA STATE PARK

⑧ **Description:** Check out the Seppmann windmill located in the park. The mill was completed in 1864 and during its peak was able to grind 150 bushels of grain a day. In 1890 a tornado claimed the windmill's arms and were never replaced. With the beautiful waterfalls of Minneopa Creek, a limestone valley, and a panoramic view of the valley, hiking in this park is a definite must.

Seasons/Hours: Memorial Day–Labor Day: 9 am–4 pm Su–Sa

Cost: Day pass: $7; annual pass: $25

Address: 54497 Gadwall Rd., Mankato, MN 56001

Phone: 507.389.5464

E-mail: info@dnr.state.mn.us

Website: www.dnr.state.mn.us/state_parks/minneopa
or www.mnrivervalley.com/sites/

Directions: From Mankato, take Hwy 169 S to Falls Area Exit (Cty Rd 69). Take a right and go two mi. Watch for signs.

Don't miss this: See the marker that commemorates Fort LeHillier, built by French explorer Pierre Charles Le Sueur in 1700. From Mankato, go two mi. S on Hwy 66.

MINNESOTA AGRICULTURAL INTERPRETIVE CENTER

⑨ **Description:** This site is home to 120 acres, representing agriculture from the 1850s to the present. You'll be able to participate in activities like churning butter, planting a garden or various other farm tasks.

Seasons/Hours: Year-round: 11 am–3 pm Tu–F

Cost: Adults: $5, youth ages 3–17: $3, children 2 and under: free

Address: 7367 300 60th Ave, Janesville, MN 56048

Phone: 507.835.2052

E-mail: farmamer@mnic.net

Website: www.farmamerica.org/

Directions: From Waseca, go four mi. W on Cty Rd 2.

R.D. HUBBARD HOUSE

⑩ **Description:** The R.D. Hubbard House was built in 1871 by the founder of the Hubbard Milling Company. This French Second Empire home restored to the 1905 era is one of the finest restoration projects in Minnesota. The house is filled with late 1800s furnishings, including Tiffany and Quetzal lights, silk wall coverings, handmade rugs, hand-painted ceilings and some original Hubbard Family pieces of furniture. Tours include the award-winning Palmer Centennial Gardens, and the carriage house which displays horse-drawn and mechanical vehicles, including an 1879 stagecoach, one of the few surviving Haynes Apperson horseless carriages and a 1926 Pontiac sports coupe.

Seasons/Hours: May-Sept: 1 pm–4 pm Sa-Su; Dec: call for weekend schedule; other times and for group tours by appointment

Cost: Adults: $2, children: $1; children under 5 and members: free

Address: 606 S Broad St, Mankato, MN 56001

Phone: 507.345.5566

E-mail: bechs@juno.com

Website: www.rootsweb.com/~mnbechs/house.html

Directions: From Hwy 169 take the Mankato/N Mankato Exit and turn left. Go over the bridge to S Broad St and turn right and go approx. five blocks to Warren St. The house is on the right side.

TREATY SITE HISTORY CENTER

⑪ *Description:*

This museum tells the story of the Dakota people and their interaction with the explorers, traders and settlers who came to the area. There is information on the Treaty of Traverse des Sioux in 1851 which opened up 24 million acres for settlement. Genealogical resources are available, and school field trips are welcome.

Treaty Site History Center

Seasons/Hours: Year-round: 10 am–4 pm Tu–Sa; 1 pm–4 pm Su

Cost: Adults: $3, children 12 and under: free

Address: 1851 N Minnesota Ave, St. Peter, MN 56082

Phone: 507.934.2160

E-mail: nchs@hickorytech.net

Directions: Located just N of St. Peter on Hwy 169.

W.W. MAYO HOUSE

⑫ *Description:*

Hand-built in 1859 by founder of the Mayo Clinic, W.W. Mayo, this Gothic-style home is where he set up his first medical practice in Minnesota. In 1874

W. W. Mayo House

Carson Nesbit Cosgrove moved into the house. Cosgrove served as the head of what is now the Green Giant Company. Take a tour and hear from guides about life as it was in the Mayo/Cosgrove home. Be sure to go next door and see "The

Mothers"—a sculpture depicting members of both families.

Seasons/Hours:	May 15–May 31: 1 p.m–4:30 pm Sa; June 1–Aug 31: 10 am–4:30 pm Tu–Sa
Cost:	Adults: $3, seniors: $2, children 6–16: $1, children 5 and under: free
Address:	118 N Main St, Le Sueur, MN 56058
Phone:	507.665.3250 or 507.665.6965
E-mail:	mayohouse@mchsi.com or mayohouse@mnhs.org
Website:	www.mayohouse.org or www.mnhs.org/places/sites/wwmh
Directions:	On Main Street of LeSueur, go ½ block N of enclosed shopping mall.

WASECA COUNTY HISTORICAL SOCIETY

(13) *Description:* The Waseca County Historical Society and museum is located in a former Methodist church in Waseca. The displays focus on the Native Americans and settlers who lived in the area. There is also an exhibit on railroading and its impact on the region. For genealogical researchers, this is a branch library of the Family History Center in Salt Lake City. Also check out their website that has a 250,000 name index and 250,000 photographs.

Seasons/Hours:	Year-round: 8 am–12 pm & 1 pm–5 pm M–F; or by appointment
Cost:	Free
Address:	315 2nd Ave NE, Waseca, MN 56093
Phone:	507.835.7700
E-mail:	director@historical.waseca.mn.us
Website:	www.historical.waseca.mn.us/
Directions:	In Waseca on 2nd Ave, one block N of Hwy 14.

WATONWAN COUNTY HISTORICAL SOCIETY & HISTORICAL CENTER

(14) *Description:* This museum has about 25 displays throughout the building, including a display of the Younger Brothers capture, a drug store, the first post office in Watonwan County, a restored log cabin and authentic horse-drawn farm equipment. The Historical Center is also home to a research library.

Seasons/Hours:	June–Sept: 9 am–11:30 pm & 1 pm–4 pm M–Th; Mar–May and Oct: 9 am–11:30 pm & 1 pm–4 pm W; closed weekends; group tours may be arranged

Cost:	Free
Address:	423 Dill Ave SW, Madelia, MN 56062
Phone:	507.642.3247
Website:	www.rootsweb.com/~mnwatonw/wchs.htm
Directions:	From Mankato, take Hwy 60 SW to Hwy 3 W to Madelia. Go W on Main St to Benzel Ave, S to 4th St then SW to Dill Ave.
Don't miss this:	A map of the county's historic places of interests is available for free by writing the society and including a self-addressed, stamped envelope.

WINNEBAGO AREA HISTORICAL SOCIETY

⑮ *Description:*	See displays and learn about the prehistoric cultures of the Blue Earth area. Visit the log cabin and reminisce about the past by viewing photographs of schools, churches, barns, Main Street and Parker College.
Seasons/Hours:	Year-round: 9 am–12 pm M–Tu; 9 am–5 pm W; 1 pm–5 pm Th & F; tours by appointment
Cost:	Free
Address:	18 1st St NE, Winnebago, MN 56098
Phone:	507.893.4660
E-mail:	wmuseum@bevcomm.net
Directions:	Take I-90 to Blue Earth, then go N on Hwy 169 to Winnebago. Exit on Cleveland Ave, and go E to 1st St NE.

END-O-LINE RAILROAD PARK AND MUSEUM

⑯ *Description:*	This is a working railroad yard complete with a rebuilt engine house, an original four-room depot, a general store, grist mill and a water tower. The turntable—built in 1901 and still operable—is the only one left in Minnesota on its original site. See a replica of the coal bunker used as a picnic shelter and interpretive area. The buildings contain various exhibits and displays of railroad artifacts, photographs, memorabilia and equipment, even an HO scale model train layout of the railroad yards in Currie. A three-mile bicycle and walking paved pathway connects the railroad park to Lake Shetek State Park.
Seasons/Hours:	Memorial Day–Labor Day: 10 am–12 pm; 1 pm–5 pm M–F; 1 pm–5 pm Sa & Su; or by appointment
Cost:	Adults: $3, students: $2; families: $10

Address:	440 N Mill St, Currie, MN 56123
Phone:	507.763.3708
E-mail:	louise@endoline.com
Website:	www.endoline.com
Directions:	From I-90 at Worthington, take Exit 43 and go 34 mi. N on Hwy 59. Turn E on Hwy 30 for four mi. In Currie, turn N on Cty Rd 38 (Mill St.) and go one mi. Park is on east side of road.
	From Marshall, go S on Hwy 59 for 26 mi. Turn E on Hwy 30 for four mi. to get to Currie.

 Murray County had the first woman sheriff in Minnesota and is the only county in the state that does not have a traffic light.

JASPER AREA HISTORICAL SOCIETY MUSEUM

⑰ *Description:*	Located in the 1889 J.M. Poorbough Building, this museum highlights the town's 105-year Jasper quarrying history. Native American artifacts, needlework and pictures are also on display at the museum.
Seasons/Hours:	Summer by appointment
Cost:	Free
Address:	217 2nd St SE, Jasper, MN 56144
Phone:	507.348.3963
Directions:	From Pipestone, take Hwy 23 S and turn left on 2nd St.

LAKE SHETEK STATE PARK

⑱ *Description:*	This site was home to a community of settlers during the 1862 Dakota Conflict. Today the park has four cabin sites and one original cabin. A brochure is available at the park office for a self-guided tour. Don't miss seeing the "Shetek"—otherwise known as the pelican—in the summer and fall. Swimming, boating, hiking, biking and more area available at the park. There are rest stops, scenic overlooks and the Shetek monument.
Seasons/Hours:	Summer: 9 am–9 pm daily
Cost:	State park annual permit: $18-$25; daily permit: $7; camping fees: $11–$18

Address:	163 State Park Rd., Currie, MN 56123
Phone:	507.763.3256
E-mail:	info@dnr.state.mn.us
Website:	www.dnr.state.mn.us/state_parks/lake_shetek/index.html
Directions:	The park is 3½ mi. NW of Currie on Cty Rd 38.

LAURA INGALLS WILDER MUSEUM AND TOURIST CENTER

⑲ *Description:*	The Laura Ingalls Wilder Museum is dedicated to the pioneer history of Laura Ingalls Wilder and all early pioneers that settled the Walnut Grove area. Six buildings make up the museum complex; come and see the quilt Laura and her daughter Rose made, along with photos of the Ingalls and Wilder families. Call ahead for staff to assist you with the use of microfilm to research ancestors from the area. The Gift Store has T-shirts, crafts and many books pertaining to the Ingalls/Wilder history. School groups can arrange for guided tours and extra activities by calling ahead.
Seasons/Hours:	April–Oct: 10 am–4 pm M–Sa; 12 pm–4 pm Su; May and Sept: 10 am–5 pm M–Sa; 12 pm–5 pm Su; June–Aug: 10 am–6 pm daily; Nov–Mar: call for information
Cost:	Adults: $4, children 6–12: $2, children 5 and under: free
Address:	330 8th St, Walnut Grove, MN 56180
Phone:	507.859.2358 or 800.528.7280
E-mail:	lauramuseum@walnutgrove.org
Website:	www.walnutgrove.org
Directions:	Museum is located ½ block S of Hwy 14 on Cty Rd 5.

LEGION PIONEER MUSEUM

⑳ *Description:*	The Legion Pioneer Museum is located in a nine-room house. The theme of four of the rooms dates back to the early twentieth century. There is a room of local history, a general store, music and information with the rest of the rooms displaying odds and ends.
Seasons/Hours:	Open by appointment only
Cost:	Free
Address:	PO Box 83, Vesta, MN 56292

Phone:	507.762.3278
Directions:	From Marshall, head E on Hwy 16 to Vesta. From Main St go two blocks N on Schley St.

LINCOLN COUNTY PIONEER MUSEUM

㉑ *Description:*	The Pioneer Museum depicts life in the late 1800s and early 1900s. There is a kitchen, sitting room, bedroom and parlor. Visit the general store, schoolhouses, a rural Icelandic church and a mail-ordered Sears, Roebuck & Co. home. See displays of buggies, farm tools and an 1872 steam engine.
Seasons/Hours:	May–Oct: 2 pm–5 pm, 7 pm–9 pm W, F & Su
Cost:	Free, donations appreciated
Address:	610 W Elm, Hendricks, MN 56136
Phone:	507.275.3537
Website:	www.ushwy75.net/citypages/hendricks/
Directions:	From I-29, take the White Exit and go E on Hwy 19 to the Hendricks sign. Turn left on Hwy 271 N to Henrdricks, then take a left on the first road in Hendricks, Cty Rd 17, that will go to the park. The museum is on the right.

LUCAN HERITAGE PARK AND MUSEUM

㉒ *Description:*	In 1976 this Chicago Northwestern Railroad Depot—believed to be one of the last in the nation of its kind—was moved to its present location to be used as a museum. Browse through a collection of John Zwach's memorabilia gathered while a member of the Minnesota House of Representatives and Minnesota Senate for a total of 40 years. The Twin Cities' first firetruck plus many more items used in the past are on display. There are also scrapbooks of Lucan organizations, newspaper clippings, local family pictures, and marriage, birth and death records.
Seasons/Hours:	Open by appointment
Cost:	Free
Address:	25558 Cty Hwy 10, Lucan, MN 56255
Phone:	507.747.2598 or 507.747.2535
Directions:	From Main St in Lucan, go ½ block E on 1st Ave.

LUND-HOEL HOUSE

㉓ Description: Built and sold by John Lund, and bought by Rev. Olaf Hoel, this 1891 Victorian home is furnished with many of the original artifacts. Postcards and books are available for sale.

Lund–Hoel House

Seasons/Hours: Memorial Day–Labor Day: 10 am–12 pm & 1 pm–5 pm M–Sa; 12 pm–5 pm Su; or by appointment

Cost: Adults: $3

Address: 101 4th St, Canby, MN 56220

Phone/Fax: Ph: 507.223.7371; Fax: 507.223.5613

Directions: Located at the intersection of Hwy 75 and 4th St N in Canby.

LYON COUNTY COURTHOUSE MUSEUM

㉔ Description: The Lyon County Courthouse was built in 1892 and is the home to the Lyon County Museum. The museum has a collection of many artifacts and exhibits that demonstrate the changes throughout the years in the homes, farms and the communities of Lyon County. Among the artifacts is the Camden Vase, believed to be 500–1,000 years old. It was found in a burial mound probably buried with a local chieftain.

Seasons/Hours: Feb–Dec: 1 pm–4 pm Tu–Sa

Address: 114 N 3rd St, Marshall, MN 56258

Phone: 507.537.6580

Directions: Located in downtown Marshall.

More than 10,000 Indian burial mounds have been found in Minnesota.

LYON COUNTY HISTORICAL SOCIETY MUSEUM

㉕ *Description:* The museum has a 1950s Schwan's Dairy Lunch ice cream and soda fountain. Also part of the museum is a Prairie Schooner, an 1872 log cabin and Native American artifacts.

Seasons/Hours: Feb–Dec: 10 am–4 pm Tu, W & F; 10 am–8 pm Th; 1 pm–4 pm Sa

Address: 114 N 3rd St, Marshall, MN 56258

Phone: 507.537.6580

Website: www.marshall-mn.org/City/museum/

Directions: Located in downtown Marshall.

MINNESOTA'S MACHINERY MUSEUM

㉖ *Description:* This is the state's largest collection of agricultural equipment and exhibits, including 1912 tractors in mint condition. The museum has six acres with five large buildings, including a farm home and a general store housing stories and artifacts from farm life. Rural art is on display along with vintage automobiles, railroad memorabilia and miniature and toy farm collections. Be sure to stop by the gift shop as well. Guided and special tours available.

Seasons/Hours: May–Sept: 10 am–4 pm M–Sa; 1 pm–4:30 pm Su

Cost: Donations

Address: Hwy 23 and Hwy 18, 1st Ave W, Hanley Falls, MN 56245

Phone/Fax: Ph: 507.768.3522; Fax: 507.768.3580

E-mail: agmuseum@frontiernet.net

Website: www.mnmachinerymuseum.com

Directions: From Granite Falls head SW on Hwy 23 to Cty Rd 18. The museum is one block W of Hwy 23 and two blocks N.

PIPESTONE COUNTY MUSEUM

㉗ Description: Located in the 1896 city hall, the Pipestone County Historical Museum is home to many exhibits. See the Native American displays of clothing, beadwork, peace pipes and weapons. Visit a general store, blacksmith shop, doctor's office and a covered wagon. The museum also has pieces of artwork by George Catlin.

Seasons/Hours: Year-round: 10 am–5 pm daily; closed holidays

Cost: General admission $3; Pipestone County Historical Society members: free

Address: 113 S Hiawatha Ave, Pipestone, MN 56164

Phone: 507.825.2563

E-mail: pipctymu@rconnect.com

Website: www.pipestoneminnesota.com/museum/

Directions: From Marshall, take Hwy 23 S, turn left on Hwy 75, then turn right on Main St E to Hiawatha Ave S. The trading post is on the corner, and the museum is just south from the post, across from the Calumet Hotel.

Don't miss this: Take a walking tour of the historic district of Pipestone, which is on the National Register of Historic Places. A brochure outlining the historic district is available at the Pipestone Area Chamber of Commerce. For more information call 800.336.6125.

PIPESTONE NATIONAL MONUMENT

㉘ Description: This park contains a visitor center with a slide show and a cultural center with a gift shop. If you enjoy crafts, be sure to catch the craft demonstrations from April to October. This site protects the pipestone quarries that were used by the Native Americans to make pipes. These pipes were used in ceremonies, religious practices and in trade. There is a ¾-mile, surfaced, self-guided trail that is handicapped accessible.

Seasons/Hours: Sept–May: 8 am–5 pm daily;
Memorial Day–Labor Day: 8 am–6 pm M–Th;
8 am–8 pm F–Su; Closed Christmas Day and New Years Day

Cost: 7-day family pass: $5; 7-day individual pass: $3; Native Americans and national park pass holders: free

Address: 36 Reservation Ave, Pipestone, MN 56164

Phone: 507.825.5464

E-mail:	alice_erickson@nps.gov
Website:	www.nps.gov/pipe
Directions:	Located on the northern edge of Pipestone. Take Hwy 75 N and follow the signs.

In 1937 the Pipestone Quarry was set aside as the first National Monument in the state.

REDWOOD COUNTY MUSEUM

㉙ Description: Once a county poor farm, then a nursing home, this complex is now home to 30 rooms worth of area history. Visitors are welcome to explore a living room, dining room, military room, general store, bridal room, doctor's office and three wildlife rooms. There is also a one-room schoolhouse on the museum grounds.

Seasons/Hours: May–Sept: 1 pm–4 pm Sa–Su; or by appointment; tours available upon request

Cost: Adults: $2, students: $1, children: 50¢

Address: 913 W Bridge St, Redwood Falls, MN 56283

Phone: 507.644.3329 or 507.627.7260

Directions: Located on Hwy 19 W.

SPIRIT OF PEACE INDIAN MUSEUM

㉚ Description: The Spirit of Peace Indian Museum and the Little Feather Center are Dakota owned and operated. Exhibits on the Dakota people promote cultural awareness. A variety of Native American exhibits explain the history of the Original Pipestone Dakota community, quarrying and pipemaking. Visitors can also listen to interpretive talks by Running Elk (Chuck Derby). Books, beadwork, jewelry and other objects are available for sale.

Seasons/Hours: Summer hours: 10 am–6 pm daily; winter hours: dependent on the weather, but usually open 12 pm–4 pm M–Sa, call ahead for specific hours

Cost: Free, donations appreciated

Address: 317 4th St NE, Pipestone, MN 56164

Phone:	507.562.1009
E-mail:	littlefeather4@hotmail.com
Website:	http://spiritofpeace.50megs.com/museum.html or http://littlefeathercenter.50megs.com/
Directions:	From Mankato, take Hwy 14 W to Florence, then turn left on Hwy 23 S into Pipestone. At the stopsign, turn right (N) and go over the railroad tracks, then left on 4th St. Go three blocks and look for the Little Feather Center on the right side.

WESTBROOK HERITAGE HOUSE MUSEUM

③① *Description:*	The Heritage House is located in the restored 1906 Westbrook Hotel. The Heritage Museum is a railroad depot that has been preserved and has the original furniture and equipment from the depot. See agricultural collections, vintage medical equipment and household items from the area.
Seasons/Hours:	June–Labor Day: 2 pm–4 pm Su; or by appointment
Cost:	Free
Write to:	Rt 1, Box 12, Westbrook, MN 56183
Phone:	507.274.6373
Directions:	From Fairmont, take I-90 W to US Hwy 71 N to US Hwy 14. Take a left on Cty Rd 6 (which turns into 5), then go W on Cty Rd 10. Take a left into Westbrook, which is visible from the road.

WHEELS ACROSS THE PRAIRIE MUSEUM

③② *Description:*	This museum features a four-unit freight train, a 1906 automobile, 1915 steam engine, a box car, caboose and tractor. See the depot where Laura Ingalls Wilder ended her trip from Walnut Grove. Other interesting sites to visit include a log cabin, schoolhouse, barber shop and post office. Children can learn through the hands-on exhibits geared especially for them. Browse through the museum's archives for research.
Seasons/Hours:	Memorial Day–Sept 4: 1 pm–5 pm; or by appointment on Su
Cost:	Adults: $2, children under 12: free
Address:	Hwy 14 W, Tracy, MN 56175
Phone:	507.629.4918
Website:	www.tracymn.com/culture.html
Directions:	On Hwy 14 on the western side of Tracy.

ANDREW J. VOLSTEAD HOUSE

⧉ Description: This is the home of US Congressman Andrew J. Volstead. The front parlor tells his life story and is dedicated to the memory of the congressman.

Seasons/Hours: Contact City Hall

Cost: Free

Address: 163 9th Ave S, Granite Falls, MN 56241

Phone: 320.564.3011

E-mail: cgf@kilowatt.net

Directions: Located at the intersection of Hwy 212 and Hwy 23 in downtown Granite Falls.

Don't miss this: The Wood Lake Battlefield and Monument was erected in 1919 on Cty Rd 18, ½ mi. W of TH 67, between Granite Falls and Echo. This monument commemorates the last battle of the Dakota Uprising of 1862—the Battle of Wood Lake—fought here Sept. 23 of that year.

 It is said that prohibitionist Andrew Volstead consumed nearly a pound of chewing tobacco a day.

ARV HUS MUSEUM

㉞ Description: Arv Hus Museum honors those of Scandinavian descent. Norwegian rosemalers are the highlight of the museum, but there are also displays on local history and culture, including local photographs of the Milan area, paintings and crafts.

Seasons/Hours: April–Dec: 10 am–4 pm Th–Su; or by appointment; group tours are available

Cost: Free

Address: Main St, PO Box 140, Milan, MN 56262

Phone: 320.734.4408 or 320.734.4829

Directions: From Hwy 12 take Hwy 59 S to intersection at Hwy 7 in Milan.

BIG STONE COUNTY HISTORICAL SOCIETY

㉟ Description: The Big Stone Historical Society has a collection of fossils 70–90 million years old. See the Muskegon, a boat that navigated Big Stone Lake until it sank in 1917. Wildlife lovers cannot miss Charles Hanson's waterfowl collection of over 500 bird specimens—one of the largest taxidermy collections in the world. There is also information on pioneer life, Big Stone Lake, and the granite industry.

Seasons/Hours: Year-round: 10 am–5 pm M–Sa; 1 pm–4 pm Su

Cost: Donation

Address: 985 Hwy 12, Ortonville, MN 56278

Phone: 320.839.3359

E-mail: chamber@bigstonelake.com

Website: www.stenseth.org/hs/bigstone2.html

Directions: In Ortonville, located at the junction of Hwy 12 and Hwy 75.

Don't miss this: The 1920 Big Stone County Courthouse at 20 SE 2nd St is listed on the National Register of Historical Places. While there, check out the war memorial on the courthouse lawn.

TRIVIA The Minnesota River flows 328 miles from Big Stone Lake to the Mississippi River.

CHIPPEWA COUNTY HISTORICAL SOCIETY

㊱ Description: The Historical Society maintains Historic Chippewa City, nestled on a 20-acre site. Today visitors can guide themselves through the 24 buildings which tell the story of pioneer life, including a general store, law office, bank and blacksmith shop. Genealogical research available at the office by appointment.

Seasons/Hours: Memorial Day–Labor Day: 9 am–5 pm M–F; 1 pm–5 pm Sa–Su & holidays; Labor Day–late-Sept: 9 am–5 pm

Cost: Chippewa City admission: adults: $4; youth ages 6–17: $2; children 5 and under: free

Address: 151 Pioneer Dr, PO Box 303, Montevideo, MN 56265

Phone: 320.269.7636

E-mail:	CCHS.June@juno.com
Website:	www.montechamber.com/cchs/cchshp.htm
Directions:	Located at intersection of Hwy 7 and Hwy 59 in Montevideo.

LAC QUI PARLE COUNTY HISTORICAL SOCIETY

(37) Description: There is much to see at this historical society; browse through the vast display of pioneer artifacts, home tools, farm implements and a doll collection. See a large animal wildlife display, Native American artifacts, a military display, a log cabin and schoolhouse with original furnishings, and a small station. Conduct research through the use of the extensive obituary files and other documentary materials available to the public.

Seasons/Hours:	May–Oct: 9 am–4:30 pm M–Sa; by appointment Su
Cost:	Museum: free, donations appreciated; $5 minimum for research
Address:	S Hwy 75, Madison, MN 56256
Phone:	320.598.7678
Website:	www.madisonmn.info/museum.html
Directions:	Located on Hwy 75 in Madison.

LAC QUI PARLE MISSION

(38) Description: Established in 1835, this wooden chapel was a WPA project that stands on the site of the original mission, overlooking the beautiful "Lake that Speaks." Inside the chapel visitors can view exhibits about the missionaries and their work, the Dakota people and Joseph Renville who was a respected trader and explorer. There are self-guided interpretive walking trails through the area where the missionaries lived.

Seasons/Hours:	May–Labor Day: 8 am–8 pm M–Su
Cost:	Free
Address:	PO Box 303, Montevideo, MN 56265
Phone:	320.269.7636
E-mail:	CCHS.June@juno.com
Website:	www.montechamber.com/cchs/lqpmissn.htm
Directions:	From Montevideo, go N on Hwy 59 six mi., then go W on Chippewa Cty Hwy 13 for 2.2 mi. Turn right at the corner; the mission is on the right.

Don't miss this: Check out the Lac Qui Parle Village and cemetery. This prairie town and its cemetery lie above the scenic Lac Qui Parle River Valley. Remnants of the Red Ox Trail and Military Trail can be seen. A marker stands near the village's first courthouse site.

RENVILLE CITY MUSEUM

(39) Description: With everything from a restored jail cell to an exhibit on area churches, variety is the spice of this museum. The life and times of Joseph Renville are also on display as well as other examples of pioneer and Dakota life.

Seasons/Hours: June–Labor Day: 1pm–4 pm Su; open during special events

Cost: Free

Address: 202 N Main St, Renville, MN 56284

Phone: 320.329.3545

Directions: From Main St in Renville, go one block N of Hwy 212.

SACRED HEART AREA MUSEUM

(40) Description: Located in a 1916 church building, this museum is home to a research library, a fine school exhibit and the history of businesses and churches of the area. Its photography exhibit with photographs and glass negatives from 1900 is quite exceptional.

Seasons/Hours: Year-round: 1:30 pm–4:30 pm Tu & Th; or by appointment; call for special events

Cost: Free

Address: 300 5th Ave, PO Box 462, Sacred Heart, MN 56285

Phone: 320.765.8868

Directions: Go to the west end of town along Hwy 212.

STONE CREEK

(41) Description: Visit this homestead on Stone Creek and explore a sod house, log cabin, secret tunnels, fishing pond and nature trails. Bring golf clubs and enjoy the three-hole golf course and driving range.

Seasons/Hours: Year-round: 2 pm–dusk M–Th; 10 am–dusk F–Su

Cost: Adults: $5; children 12 and under: $3

Address:	9017 Hwy 40 NW, Montevideo, MN 56265
Phone:	320.793.6783 or (877) 285.6202
Directions:	Take Hwy 7 to Montevideo, then Hwy 277 N to Hwy 29 W. This homestead is at the intersection off Hwy 29 and Hwy 40.

SWENSSON FARM MUSEUM

(42) *Description:*	Come visit the home of Norwegian Olof Swensson, one of Minnesota's most innovative immigrants. Today visitors are welcome to explore his 17-acre farmstead with its 22-room brick farm building, a very unique timber-framed barn, grist mill, family burial plot and pole building. Be sure to check out the chapel on this self-guided tour.
Seasons/Hours:	Memorial Day–Labor Day: 1 pm–5 pm Su; or by appointment
Cost:	Adults: $4, youth ages 6–17: $2, children 5 and under: free
Mailing Address:	PO Box 303, Montevideo, MN 56265
Phone:	320.269.7636
E-mail:	CCHS.June@juno.com
Website:	www.montechamber.com/cchs/swensson.htm
Directions:	Go six mi. E of Montevideo on Hwy 7, then five mi. S on Cty Rd 6 and ⅛ mi. E on Cty Rd 15.

TRIVIA

As the 5th largest dairy producer in the country, Minnesota produces approximately 9.7 billion pounds of milk each year. Hence, the state drink is milk.

UPPER SIOUX AGENCY

(43) *Description:*	This historic site has been reconstructed. It was an 1854 employee duplex for the Indian agency, and was destroyed during the 1862 Dakota Conflict. The park has a wide range from knolls to bluffs to wooded slopes. Come enjoy the many activities for all seasons.
Seasons/Hours:	Year-round: 8 am–10 pm daily
Cost:	State park permit: $12-$25; day-use sticker: $7; camping fees: $11–$20
Address:	5908 Hwy 67, Granite Falls, MN 56241

Phone:	320.564.4777
Directions:	From the Granite Falls intersection of Hwy 212 and Hwy 23, go S one block to Hwy 67 and turn left. Go eight mi. to park entrances.
Don't miss this:	Go two mi. S on Cty Rd 18 from the park to the Wood Lake Battlefield Monument, which was erected in 1919. This monument commemorates the Battle of Wood Lake, fought there September 23, 1862. This was the last battle of the Dakota Uprising of 1862.

YELLOW MEDICINE COUNTY HISTORICAL MUSEUM

㊹ *Description:*	This museum specializes in local county history, featuring two special exhibits: the 8,000-year-old bison bones and the oldest exposed granite rock. Also see artifacts from American Indians and pioneers. Check for their special events during the summer.
Seasons/Hours:	Memorial Day–Oct 1: 11 am–5 pm Th–Su
Cost:	Free
Address:	Jct Hwy 67 and 23, PO Box 145, Granite Falls, MN 56241
Phone:	320.564.4479
Website:	www.kilowatt.net/ymchs/default.htm
Directions:	From Montevideo, go S on Hwy 42 to the intersection of Hwy 67 and Hwy 23.

AUGUST SCHELL BREWERY

㊺ *Description:*	This 1860 brewery and museum has its antique brewing equipment on display, as well as of the history of brewing and of the Schell family. There are also gardens and a deer park, open 8 am to dusk for public viewing.
Seasons/Hours:	Memorial Day–Labor Day: 12 pm–5 pm daily; tours: 3 pm & 4 pm M–F; 1, 2, 3 & 4 pm Sa & Su
Address:	1860 Shell Rd., New Ulm, MN 56073
Phone/Fax:	Ph: 507.354.5528 or 800.770.5020; Fax: 507.359.9119
E-mail:	schells@schellsbrewery.com
Website:	www.schellsbrewery.com
Directions:	From Hwy 169, take the St. Peter Exit 99 to Nicollet and to Hwy 14. Take the New Ulm Exit Hwy 39, go left to the first set of stoplights, turn right and go two blocks. Watch for signs.

Minnesota faced its worst grasshopper plague in 1873. For five summers, the grasshoppers ate everything in their paths—from crops and trees to clothes and gardens.

BIRCH COULEE BATTLEFIELD AND MONUMENT

(46) Description: One of the worst battles of the U.S–Dakota Conflict took place on this site in 1862. Visitors can walk the trails and learn what happened here with guide posts throughout the trail. In 1894 two monuments were erected nearby, one honoring the soldiers and one honoring the Dakota Warriors.

Seasons/Hours: May–Oct: dawn until dusk daily

Cost: Free

Address: c/o Lower Sioux Agency Historic Site, 32469 Cty Hwy 2, Morton, MN 56270

Phone: 507.697.6321

E-mail: birchcoulee@mnhs.org

Website: www.mnhs.org/places/sites/bc/index.html

Directions: From Morton, go three mi. N on Hwy 71 to the intersection of Hwy 2 and Hwy 18, then go one mi. E.

BROWN COUNTY HISTORICAL SOCIETY

(47) Description: The Brown County Historical Society is located in a German Renaissance-style building, built in 1910. It has been the home to the society since 1984. Check out pioneer and Native American life in multiple exhibits on the museum's three floors.

Seasons/Hours: Year-round: 9 am–4 pm M–F; 1 pm–5 pm Sa

Cost: Adults: $2, students: free

Address: 2 N Broadway, New Ulm, MN 56073

Phone/Fax: Ph: 507.233.2616; Fax: 507.354.1068

E-mail: bchs@newulmtel.net

Website: www.BrownCountyHistoryMNUSA.org

Directions: From Minneapolis, S on US 169 to W MN 99. Right on US 14, left on MN 15, left on Center St.

Don't miss this: While visiting the society, be sure to get a brochure to begin a walking tour of New Ulm. The tour will take visitors throughout the city passing 38 historic sites.

CATHEDRAL OF THE HOLY TRINITY

(48) Description: The current cathedral was started in 1890 and finished in 1901. The original church was built in 1858 and destroyed during the Dakota Uprising of 1862. The second building was completed in 1869 but was destroyed by a tornado.

Seasons/Hours: Year-round: 8 am–4:30 pm M–F

Cost: Free

Address: 605 N State St, New Ulm, MN 56073

Phone/Fax: Ph: 507.354.4158; Fax: 507.354.2563

E-mail: newulmcathedral@hotmail.com

Website: www.cathedralht.org

Directions: From Hwy 169 in Mankato, head W on Hwy 14 to New Ulm. Continue from Hwy 14 to 7th St N, to N State St. then turn left one block.

FLANDRAU STATE PARK

(49) Description: Many of the buildings on this site were constructed by the Works Progress Administration (WPA) in the 1930s. During the 1940s the group center was used to house German Prisoners of War. Today the park offers a sand-bottom swimming pond, picnic areas, campground and a group center. There are many great places for hiking during the warmer months and cross-country skiing during the winter.

Seasons/Hours: Memorial Day–Labor Day: 9 am–9 pm daily

Cost: Day passes: $4; annual passes: $25

Address: 1300 Summit Ave, New Ulm, MN 56073

Phone/Fax: Ph: 507.233.9800; Fax: 507.359.1544

E-mail: info@dnr.state.mn.us

Website: www.dnr.state.mn.us/state_parks/flandrau

Directions: In New Ulm, follow Broadway (Hwy 15) to 10th St S. Proceed W on 10th St S up the hill to Summit Ave. Turn left heading S and go three blocks to the park entrance which will be on the right (west) side of Summit Ave. Park entrance is next to the New Ulm Country Club.

(49) Description: Originally built as a police station, this fort went on to be the site of two major battles in the Dakota Conflict. Today visitors can explore many exhibits depicting the history of the fort and the conflict. The site is also home to a nine-hole golf course, lots of trails in addition to plenty of fishing and camping opportunities.

Fort Ridgely

Minnesota Historical Society

Seasons/Hours: May–Labor Day: 10 am–5 pm F & Sa; 12 pm–5 pm Su

Cost: State park permit: $12-$20; day-use sticker: $4; camping fees: $7-$14.50; museum is free

Address: 72404 Cty Rd 30, Fairfax, MN 55332

Phone: 507.426.7888, 507.697.6321 or 888.PAST.FUN (888.727.8386)

E-mail: ftridgely@mnhs.org

Website: www.mnhs.org/places/sites/fr/

Directions: The fort is located in Fort Ridgely State Park. The park is off Hwy 4, seven mi. S of Fairfax.

Don't miss this: Red Rock Trading Post Site. Fur trader Joseph La Framoise established this trading post in 1834, located four mi. SE of Fort Ridgely.

TRIVIA Renville's county seat, Olivia, is the Corn Capital of Minnesota. A monument was erected in 1973 to pay tribute to this title.

GILFILLAN ESTATE

(51) Description: This 1882 estate was home to two generations of Charles Gilfillans. Both were very active philanthropists in the Redwood County area. Charles Duncan played a pivotal role in establishing a safe and sufficient water supply in St. Paul and served on a committee which erected a monument at Birch Coulee. His son, Charles Oswinn, helped set up several programs that helped people with medical expenses. Browse through the farm site, which now holds a wonderful collection of early farming equipment and antiques.

Seasons/Hours: June–Labor Day: 1 pm–4:30 pm Sa and Su; or by appointment

Cost: Adults: $5 for full tour, house and summer kitchen: $3, children: $2

Address: Hwy 67, Morgan, MN 56270

Mailing Address: Lorraine Tauer, Box 147, Morgan, MN 56266

Phone: 507.249.3451

Directions: Located on Hwy 67, SE of Redwood Falls.

HARKIN STORE

(52) Description: Area settlers would get their supplies, mail and gossip all at this store, but after grasshoppers brought agricultural failure, the store was forced to close. Today visitors can once again gather at the store to play checkers, relax on the porch or check out the abandoned shelves full of original 1870s provisions. Costumed interpreters are on site to answer any questions. Educational programs run most Sunday afternoons in summer months. Call ahead for details.

Tim Rummelhoff, courtesy Minnesota Historical Society

Harkin Store

Seasons/Hours: May: 10 am–5 pm Sa & Su; June–Aug: 10 am–5 pm Tu–Su; Sept: 10 am–5 pm Sa & Su; first two weekends in Oct: 10 am–5 pm F–Su

Cost:	Adults: $2; children under 13: free; different fees may apply for special events
Mailing Address:	PO Box 112, New Ulm, MN 56073
Phone:	507.354.8666 or 507.934.2160
E-mail:	harkinstore@mnhs.org
Website:	www.mnhs.org/places/sites/hs/
Directions:	From New Ulm, go nine mi. NW on Cty Rd 21.

HERMANN'S MONUMENT

㊳ *Description:*	This 102-foot monument was erected to the soldier, Hermann. According to Roman historians, he was an ancient commander who led German tribes in defeating a 25,000 soldier army of the widespread Roman Empire, a victory that was one of the worst the Romans had ever suffered. The legend of Hermann was widespread, standing for fidelity, freedom and honor for all Germans. In 1887 the fraternal society, the "Order of the Sons of Hermann," commissioned this monument to be erected.
Seasons/Hours:	Memorial Day–Labor Day: 10 am–4 pm M–F; 10 am–7 pm Sa & Su
Cost:	$1
Address:	Center St and Monument St, New Ulm, MN 56073
Phone:	507.359.8344
Website:	www.newulmweb.com/citylights/hermann.html or www.new-ulm.mn.us
Directions:	Off Broadway in New Ulm, take Center St W to Monument St. Monument is in Hermann Heights Park.

JEFFERS PETROGLYPHS

㊴ *Description:*	This site is home to 2,000 early Native American carvings dating from 3000 BC through the Late Woodland Period of 900–1750 AD. The carvings—created using chisels made of stone or antlers—depict shamans and other human figures, animals, important events and sacred ceremonies. Markers will informatively guide you along 1.2 miles of trails through the prairie. The visitor center has exhibits on the petroglyphs and daily programs for kids.
Seasons/Hours:	May and Sept: 10 am–5 pm F–Sa; 12 pm–5 pm Su; Memorial Day–Labor Day: 10 am–5 pm M–F; 10 am–8pm Sa, 12pm–8pm Su Oct–April: by reservation

Cost:	Adults: $5; seniors: $4; children 6 to 12: $3, children 6 and under and MHS members: free
Address:	27160 Cty Rd 2, Comfrey, MN 56019
Phone:	507.628.5591
E-mail:	jefferspetroglyphs@mnhs.org
Website:	www.mnhs.org/places/sites/jp
Directions:	Go three mi. E of Hwy 71 on Cty Rd 10, then one mi. S on Cty Rd 2.

Jeffers Petroglyphs

LIND HOUSE

(55) *Description:*	The Lind House was built in 1887 for Minnesota's 14th governor, John Lind. See the beautiful Queen Anne architecture, furnishings from the family and an original oil painting of Governor Lind.
Seasons/Hours:	Jan–Mar: appointment only; April–May: 1 pm–4 pm F–Su; June–Aug: 1 pm–4 pm daily; Sept–Nov: 1 pm–4 pm F–Su
Cost:	$1
Address:	622 Center St, New Ulm, MN 56073
Phone:	507.354.8802
Website:	www.lindhouse.homestead.com
Directions:	Located on the corner of State St and Center St, one block W of Hwy 14/15 on Center St.

56 **Description:** Through videos, exhibits and interpretive trails, visitors will learn more about the Dakota way of life and the U.S.–Dakota Conflict of 1862. There is an interpretive center that goes into great detail about the what led to the conflict and what happened after.

Minnesota Historical Society

Seasons/Hours: May–Labor Day: 10 am–5 pm M–Sa; 12 pm–5 pm Su; Labor Day–Oct: 1 pm–5 pm Sa & Su

Cost: Adults: $4; seniors: $3; children 6-12: $2; children 6 and under and MHS members: free

Lower Sioux Agency

Address: 32469 Redwood Cty Hwy 2, Morton, MN 56270

Phone: 507.697.6321 or 888.PAST.FUN

E-mail: lowersioux@mnhs.org

Website: www.mnhs.org/places/sites/lsa/

Directions: Watch for signs as you head eight mi. E of Redwood Falls on Cty Hwy 2.

MCCONE SOD HOUSES

57 **Description:** Experience the lifestyle of Laura Ingalls Wilder as you visit these unique prairie sod homes. The dugout is simply furnished and surrounded by restored prairie grasses and wildflowers. Reminiscent of those "Little House on the Prairie" days, the prairie soddy is decorated with the charm of the 1880s homesteader era. This is a popular destination for a field trip or an overnight stay at the bed and breakfast.

Seasons/Hours: April–Oct: 10 am–5 pm daily

Cost: Adults: $3, children under 7: free

Address:	12598 Magnolia Ave, Sanborn, MN 56083
Phone:	507.723.5138
Website:	www.sodhouse.org
Directions:	18 mi. E of Walnut Grove, one mi. E from the intersection of Hwy 14 and Hwy 71, follow the signs, then turn on Magnolia.

MCLEOD COUNTY HERITAGE AND CULTURAL CENTER

58 *Description:*	The McLeod County Heritage and Cultural Center is dedicated to the late wildlife artist Les Kouba, complete with a gallery showing many of his prints and awards. Other exhibits display artifacts of early pioneer life, the Civil War, agriculture and Native American arrowheads. Genealogical research materials include microfilms of county census records and newspapers. Family histories and indexed newspaper articles are also available.
Seasons/Hours:	Year-round: 10 am–8 pm M; 10 am–4:30 pm Th & F; 1 pm–4 pm Sa
Cost:	Adults: $3, seniors: $2, students: $1, children 6 & under: free
Address:	380 School Rd N, Hutchinson, MN 55350
Phone:	320.587.2109
E-mail:	asa@hutchtel.net
Website:	www.mcleodhistory.org
Directions:	From Hutchinson, take Hwy 7 W to the School Rd intersection.

RENVILLE COUNTY MUSEUM

59 *Description:*	Visitors will find a main museum building containing early Native American history and artifacts, a parlor, dining and kitchen scene, as well as two early schoolhouses, a blacksmith shop, a log cabin built in 1869 by Scandinavian pioneers and a farm machinery building. One schoolhouse is full Red Wing pottery, dishes, Depression and Japanese glassware, toys, clothes and other various collections, while the other has been restored as a schoolhouse in its original state.
Seasons/Hours:	May–Sept: 10 am–4 pm Tu–Sa; 1 pm–4 pm Su; Oct–April: 10 am–4 pm Tu–F
Cost:	Adults: $2, children under 12 and Historical Society Members: free

Address:	441 N Park Dr, Morton, MN 56270
Phone:	507.697.6147
E-mail:	rchs@rconnect.com
Website:	www.rootsweb.com/~mnrenvil/mus-rchs.htm
Directions:	In Morton follow Hwy 19 to Park Dr. Turn N and the museum will be on the east side of the road. Follow signs.

SIBLEY COUNTY HISTORICAL SOCIETY

⑥⓪ *Description:*	The Sibley County Historical Society is located in the A.F. Poehler home. The home was built in 1885 and has been preserved throughout the years. It displays the latest features of the 1880s, such as an upstairs bathroom and central heat. An 1858 log cabin that was built by Christian Didra, an immigrant from Germany is in the backyard.
Seasons/Hours:	Memorial Day–Oct: 2 pm–5 pm Su; tours available by appointment
Cost:	$2 per person
Write to:	PO Box 407, Henderson, MN 56044
Phone:	507.248.3434
E-mail:	hapander@spacestar.net
Website:	www.history.sibley.mn.us/
Directions:	Located in Henderson on Cty Rd 19.

SLEEPY EYE DEPOT MUSEUM

⑥① *Description:*	The Sleepy Eye Museum is located in a 1902 depot. The original Sleepy Eye Depot was built in 1872 but burned down only five years later. This second depot, now on the National Register of Historic Places, was built in 1887 and was used until the early 1980s. The museum houses artifacts from the area including the Sleepy Eye Drum and Bugle Corps' uniforms, photos and instruments. There is also a monument for Chief Sleepy Eye.
Seasons/Hours:	May–Dec: 10 am–4 pm Tu–Sa; or by appointment
Cost:	Free
Address:	100 Oak St NW, Sleepy Eye, MN 56085
Phone:	507.794.5053

E-mail:	depot@SleepyEyetel.net
Directions:	From Hwy 14 in Sleepy Eye, go N on 1st Ave one block to Oak St.

WANDA GAG HOUSE

(62) *Description:*	See the house where writer and illustrator Wanda Gag grew up. After the death of her parents, she sold her works to support her family. This eventually lead to the creation of her most popular book, *Millions of Cats.*
Seasons/Hours:	June–Aug: 1 pm–4 pm Sa & Su; or by appointment
Cost:	$1 suggested donation
Address:	226 N Washington, PO Box 432, New Ulm, MN 56073
Phone:	507.359.2632
Website:	www.newulmweb.com/citylights/gag/gag.htm
Directions:	From Hwy 169, go to St. Peter and take Hwy 99 through Nicollet to Hwy 14 into New Ulm. Take a left, still on Hwy 14, to the first stoplight and go right to the 3rd N. Between 2nd and 3rd watch for a sign, go left and come up two blocks.
Don't miss this:	Eight mi. W of New Ulm on Cty Rd 29 is the Milford Township Monument, which memorializes the 52 Milford settlers killed during the Dakota Conflict of 1862.

ATWATER AREA HISTORICAL SOCIETY

(63) *Description:*	This museum is dedicated to preserving local history. It is housed in an old bank building with exhibits and countless photographs showing rural area life. Don't miss their military uniform display.
Seasons/Hours:	Year-round: 1 pm–4 pm M–F; 10 am–12 p.m, 1 pm–4 pm Sa
Cost:	Free
Address:	108 3rd St N, Atwater, MN 56209
Phone:	320.974.8284
E-mail:	kandhist@wecnet.com
Directions:	From Main St in Atwater, go three blocks W on Atlantic and turn N on 3rd St.

GRAND ARMY OF THE REPUBLIC HALL

(64) Description: The Meeker County Historical Society Museum and the Frank Daggett Post #35 Grand Army of the Republic (G.A.R.) Hall reflect the diverse history of the county. The G.A.R. was organized in 1866 and its membership was limited to veterans of the Union Army of the Civil War. This hall, listed on the National Register of Historic Places, is one of very few left in the nation. Learn about Frank Daggett, a local newspaper publisher who commanded two all-African-American heavy artillery regiments in the Civil War, and Albert Van Spence, a black member of the Daggett Post who returned to Minnesota with Daggett after the War. Find Indian artifacts, an early log cabin, a blacksmith shop, implements of farm and village life and much more.

Seasons/Hours: Year-round: 12 pm–4 pm Tu–Su

Cost: Donation

Address: 308 N Marshall Ave, Litchfield, MN 55355

Phone: 320.693.8911

E-mail: webbie@hutchtel.net

Website: www.litch.com/gar/Index.html

Directions: Litchfield is at the intersection of Hwy 12 and Hwy 22, 40 mi. S of St. Cloud. The G.A.R. Hall and Museum is just E of Central Park.

GROVE CITY MUSEUM

(65) Description: Maintained by the Grove City Area Historical Society, this park features the Old Wind Mill which was constructed in 1879.

Seasons/Hours: Year-round: 11 am–4 pm Tu & Th or by appointment

Cost: Free

Address: 205 3rd S St, Grove City, MN 56243

Write to: Grove City Area Historical Society, PO Box 145, Grove City, MN 56243-0145

Phone: 320.857.9450

E-mail: lindstromd@willmar.com

Directions: One block N of Hwy 12 on North 2nd Street.

Don't miss this: The Grove Mill City Park, North 2nd Street, is home to the Old Wind Mill. Constructed in 1879, it is maintained by the Grove City Area Historical Society. Open year round, but to get inside the structure, contact the city clerk 320.857.2263.

The Acton Monument, the site of an 1862 Indian Massacre, is located on a homestead 5 mi south of Grove City.

TRIVIA Minnesota's waterways flow in three different directions: northward to Hudson Bay, eastward to the Atlantic Ocean and southward to the Gulf of Mexico.

KANDIYOHI COUNTY HISTORICAL SOCIETY AND MUSEUM

66 *Description:* The Society maintains a depot, a school built in 1880 and the 1893 Sperry House. This house contains some of the original contents including a sewing rocker, bedroom set and an old buggy. The depot is home to a 1929 P-2 class locomotive.

Seasons/Hours: Year-round: 9 am–5 pm M–F; also Memorial Day–Labor Day: 1 pm–5 pm Sa & Su

Cost: Free

Address: 610 NE Business 71, Willmar, MN 56201

Phone: 320.235.1881

E-mail: kandhist@wecnet.com

Website: www.freepages.genealogy.rootsweb.com/~kchs123/

Directions: From Hwy 12, go NE on Lakeland Dr, turn left on High Ave then turn right on Puerto Rico St. Turn right on Homewood Ave (Hwy 71).

Don't miss this: While at the Historical Society pick up a brochure to guide you in a self tour of historical sites. There are 21 sites along the route, including the 1858 Endreson log cabin where Guri Endreson saved three men during the 1862 Conflict. Experience Robbins Island, which provided refuge for many people from fires and enemies.

MONSON LAKE STATE PARK

67 *Description:* Monson Lake was the site of one of the first confrontations of the U.S.–Dakota Conflict of 1862. The state park is dedicated to two Swedish immigrant families, the Brobergs, who were killed on August 20th. An account of the only two survivors, 16-year-old Anna Broberg and her cousin Peter, can be seen at the park office. Check out the beautiful wildlife, go fishing, bird watching or just hike through the 187-acre park.

Seasons/Hours:	Year-round: 8 am–10 pm daily; park office: Memorial Day–Labor Day; call for park office hours
Cost:	Day pass: $7; annual pass: $20
Address:	1690 15th St NE, Sunburg, MN 56289
Phone:	320.366.3797
Directions:	20 mi. NW of Willmar. Access is off Hwy 9, 1½ mi. W of Sunburg via Cty Rd 95.

OLD DEPOT MUSEUM

(68) *Description:*	Ride in the caboose, climb the Wm. Crooks locomotive, ring the train bell, hide in the boxcar. These are just a few of the activities that make a visit to the Old Depot Museum fun and exciting. With two floors of train memorabilia to see, pictures of train travel and an abundance of reference material dedicated to railroading, one gets the feel of what it was like when rail transportation was at its peak.
Seasons/Hours:	June–Sept: 10 am–4:30 pm daily
Cost:	Adults: $2.50, children: $1
Address:	651 Hwy 12. W, Dassel, MN 55325
Phone:	320.275.3876
Directions:	From Minneapolis, go 50 mi. W on Hwy 12.

SIBLEY STATE PARK

(69) *Description:*	In 1935 the Veterans' Conservation Corps moved into the park for three years to build roads and trails that can still be enjoyed today. Visitors can hike up Mount Tom, then take a swim and go fishing or boating on Lake Andrew. Camping is also available.
Seasons/Hours:	Year-round: 8 am–10 pm daily; call for office hours
Cost:	12-month permit: $25; daily permit: $7; camping fees: $11–$18
Address:	800 Sibley Park Rd NE, New London, MN 56273-9664
Phone:	320.354.2055
E-mail:	info@dnr.state.mn.us
Website:	www.dnr.state.mn.us/state_parks/sibley/index.html
Directions:	From St. Cloud, take Hwy 23 to New London, then Hwy 9 W two blocks to Cty Rd 40 and turn left. Go to Hwy 71 then go one mi. N to park entrance.

SWIFT COUNTY HISTORICAL MUSEUM

70 **Description:** This museum depicts local county history through artifacts from the area, including an authentic log cabin and a Viking axe that was found on a nearby farm. Exhibits tell the history of the last five decades of the twentieth century in the county. The museum also has an excellent library for genealogy research.

Seasons/Hours: Year-round: 10 am–4:30 pm Tu–F; 10 am–3 pm Sa; or by appointment

Cost: Free

Address: 2135 Minnesota Ave #2, W Hwy 12, Benson, MN 55063

Phone: 320.843.4467

E-mail: historical.society@co.swift.mn.us

Directions: Located in Benson on W Hwy 12.

BLUE MOUNDS STATE PARK

71 **Description:** This state park was named for a large outcropping first known as "The Mound." In the mid-1800s it appeared blue to the settlers traveling westward, who named the landmark the Blue Mound. Visitors can hike to the Mound's southern end to see the mysterious 1,250-foot long line of rocks aligned in an east-to-west direction. On the first day of spring and fall, the sunrise and sunset are lined up on this stone alignment. The Frederick Manfred Home serves as the visitor center for this state park, which was built into the prairie.

Seasons/Hours: Year-round: dawn to dusk

Cost: 12-month permit: $25; daily permit: $7; camping fees: $11–$18

Write to: Rt 1, Box 52, Luverne, MN 56156

Phone/Fax: Ph: 507.283.1307; Fax: 507.283.1306

Website: www.dnr.state.mn.us/state_parks/blue_mounds/index.html

Directions: From the town of Luverne, go N four mi. on Hwy 75. Turn E on Cty Rd 20 and go one mi. to park entrance.

TRIVIA Rock County has no lakes.

COTTONWOOD COUNTY HISTORICAL SOCIETY

72 **Description:** The Cottonwood County Historical Society was first established in 1901. The museum has exhibits chronicling the development of the county from the Native Americans to the early twentieth century. There are agricultural displays depicting the early times of the county along with an early settler's home, schoolhouse and a general store. The Remick Art Gallery showcases local artists in the county through changing exhibits throughout the year. This handicapped accessible museum is also home to a research library specializing in county and family histories.

Hours: 8 am–4 pm M–F; tours by appointment

Cost: Free; $2 for research

Address: 812 4th Ave, Windom, MN 56101

Phone: 507.831.1134

E-mail: cchs@rrcnet.org

Website: www.rootsweb.com/~mncotton/cchs.htm

Directions: Go two blocks W of Hwy 60 and Hwy 71 intersection in downtown Windom. Museum is at 8th St and 4th Ave intersection.

FAIRMONT OPERA HOUSE

73 **Description:** Built in 1901, the Fairmont Opera House has been completely restored and is listed in the National Register of Historic Places. This is Fairmont's gathering place for entertainment, meetings, dances and other events.

Seasons/Hours: Year-round; call ahead for performances

Cost: Varies by performance; call ahead for admission prices

Address: 45 Downtown Plaza, PO Box 226, Fairmont, MN 56031

Phone: 507.238.4900

E-mail: opera@bevcomm.net

Website: www.fairmont.org/foh/home.htm

Directions: Located in downtown Fairmont.

⑭ Description: Step into the history of the pioneers of Southwest Minnesota as you visit this park in Jackson. Fort Belmont, classified as a civilian fort, was constructed and occupied by settlers after returning to the area they fled from

Fort Belmont

during a massacre of the Dakota Uprising of 1862. Within this park see an 1873 farmhouse, a 100-year-old church, a log cabin and stockade, a blacksmith shop, a sod house, a gift shop and more. Call for more information on special events at Fort Belmont.

Seasons/Hours: Memorial Day–Labor Day: 10 a.m–4 pm M–Sa; 12 pm–4 pm Su; tours by appointment

Cost: Adults: $3, children age 10 & over: $1.50; children under 10: free with a paid adult

Address: Hwy 71 S, Jackson, MN 56143

Phone: 507.847.3867

E-mail: chamber@cityofjacksonmn.com

Directions: From I-90 take Exit 73 and turn S onto Hwy 71. Go to the first intersection, turn and go W about ½ mi.

HINKLY HOUSE MUSEUM

⑮ Description: This is a late nineteenth century Victorian home that was built with native quartzite. It took six months for Knute Steine to head two large crews of carpenters and stone masons to build the home, which includes 12 rooms, two bathrooms, a full basement and full attic with a cupola. This museum holds original furnishings to the house, as well as period antiquities.

Seasons/Hours: June–Aug: 2 pm–4 pm Tu, Th, Sa; or by appointment

Cost: Free will donations (based on what it is worth to the visitors)

Address: 217 Freeman Ave N, Luverne, MN 56156

Phone: 507.449.2115

Website:	www.luvernemn.com/hinkly-house.htm
Directions:	From I-90, take the Luverne Exit N to Hwy 75 and go two blocks N past the stoplight. Turn E (right) on Luverne Ave, museum is on the corner lot.
Don't miss this:	Go to the Chamber of Commerce at 102 E Main St for booklets on a walking tour of Luverne.

JACKSON COUNTY HISTORICAL MUSEUM

⑦⑥ *Description:*	See the Heron Lake Display, depicting Heron Lake from 1887 to the present day and includes a waterfowl egg collection from the early 1900s. Walk down Main Street, Jackson County, as it was to first pioneers. Pass by the bank, general store, barber shop, post office, shoe shop, hat shop and more. A miniature farm—carved and built by S. Berkness, a pioneer of Heron Lake—shows what a farm was like before and after the dawn of electricity upon these dwellings in the 1930s. The Historical Society grants public access to county cemetery records, newspaper microfilm, area picture postcards and books.
Seasons/Hours:	Winter: 10 am–4 pm Tu & Th; summer: 10 am–4 pm M–F
Cost:	Museum is free; $5 and nominal fees for research
Address:	307 Hwy 86, Lakefield, MN 56150
E-mail:	jchs@frontiernet.net
Directions:	Located W of Hwy 86 in Lakefield.

JACKSON COUNTY FAIR VILLAGE

⑦⑦ *Description:*	Explore a log cabin, schoolhouse, farm, church and business buildings as they may have looked in their prime.
Seasons/Hours:	Open during the county fair; Aug–Labor Day: 11 am–7 pm; other times by appointment
Address:	Jackson County Fairgrounds, Jackson, MN 56143
Phone:	507.847.2402
E-mail:	champel@unitedprairiebank.com
Directions:	Located at the intersection of W Ashley St and Cty Rd 51.
Don't miss this:	A granite shaft was built in Ashley Park in 1909, to memorialize 19 pioneer settlers killed in this area in 1857 and 1862.

LINCOLN PARK

78 Description: William Robert Livingston came with his wife to Martin County in 1866. They settled in Silver Lake Township and built their homestead, which they named "Tall Oak." See this log cabin in Fairmont's Lincoln Park.

Seasons/Hours: Year-round: daily; cabin is open in the summertime, call 507.238. 9461 for hours

Cost: Free

Address: 1300 N North Ave, Lincoln Park, Fairmont, MN 56031

Phone/Fax: Ph: 507.235.5178; Fax: 507.235.5179

E-mail: mchs@bevcomm.net

Website: www.fairmont.org/docs/fmtsites.htm

Directions: From I-90, exit at Hwy 15 and go S. Turn right on Winnebago Ave, and keep going W eight blocks to the end of the street. The cabin is in Lincoln Park.

MARTIN COUNTY COURTHOUSE

79 Description: This example of classical-style architecture was dedicated in 1907 and is now on the National Register of Historic Places. It was constructed of Marquette rain-drop sandstone from Michigan and Buff-Bedford limestone from Indiana. The dome extends 58 feet above the roof, rising 108 feet from the ground.

Seasons/Hours: Year-round: 8 am–5 pm M–F; or by appointment

Cost: Free

Address: 201 Lake Ave, Fairmont, MN 56031

Phone: 507.238.3126

Website: www.fairmont.org/docs/fmtsites.htm

Directions: From I-90, Go S on Hwy 15 to Fairmont. Turn W on Blue Earth Ave and go to Lake Ave intersection.

MARTIN COUNTY HISTORICAL SOCIETY

80 Description: Organized in 1929, the Martin County Historical Society is currently located in a school with a living room and cooking area from the late 1800s, a military room with military memorabilia, dolls of the 1800s, farm implements from the early 1900s, a 1923 LaFrance firetruck, a 1912 motorcycle and Native American artifacts.

Seasons/Hours:	Year-round: 8:30 am–12 pm, 1 pm–4:30 pm M–F; special tours and appointments on Sa
Cost:	Free
Address:	304 E Blue Earth Ave, Fairmont, MN 56031
Phone/Fax:	Ph: 507.235.5178; Fax: 507.235.5179
E-mail:	mchs@bevcomm.net
Website:	www.co.martin.mn.us/mchs/index
Directions:	From I-90, take Hwy 15 S to Blue Earth Ave Go E on Blue Earth Ave to the 7th block. The pioneer museum is on the south side at the intersection of Elm St and Blue Earth Ave.

MURRAY COUNTY HISTORICAL SOCIETY AND MUSEUM

⑧⑴ *Description:*	This site is home to over 10,000 artifacts, an old country store display, a 1912 Ford Model T Runabout, a replica of the Immanuel Lutheran Church from Avoca including interior furnishings, an electrostatic machine and other medical paraphernalia. Nearby the museum is the Wornson Cabin, built in 1872 from local oak. Browse through agricultural machinery and tools and see the 1926 Caterpillar 60. Find a wealth of material in the museum's research center—microfilms of census records, county newspapers, family files, local history books and scrapbooks, plat books and school yearbooks.
Seasons/Hours:	Feb–Mar: 10 am–5 pm Tu, W & Th; Apr–Dec: 10 am–5 pm M–F (plus 1 pm–5 pm Sa during summer); tours and other times by appointment
Cost:	Free
Address:	2480 29th St, PO Box 61, Slayton, MN 56172
Phone:	507.836.6533
E-mail:	society@frontiernet.net
Website:	www.rootsweb.com/~mnmurray/sources.htm#museum
Directions:	In Slayton, go S of the County Government Center and Courts Building to the north side of the fairgrounds.

NOBLES COUNTY HISTORICAL SOCIETY MUSEUM

 Description: This society has artifacts pertaining to Nobles County, displayed in exhibits that rotate throughout the year. Extensive geneology research is also available.

Seasons/Hours: Year-round: 1 pm–5 pm M–F

Cost: Free

Address: 407 12th St, Worthington, MN 56187

Phone: 507.376.4431

E-mail: nchs@frontiernet.net

Website: www.stenseth.org/hs/nobles.html

Directions: From I-90 W take Exit 42 (Diagonal Rd.) and go S (left) on 10th Ave, then right on 10th St and left on 4th Ave. The museum is located in the lower level of the County Library.

NOBLES COUNTY PIONEER VILLAGE

 Description: The Pioneer Village is typical of many small, Midwestern communities at the beginning of the twentieth century. Visitors can see antique farm equipment, a train depot, farm house, gas station, hospital, church and graveyard, sod house, blacksmith shop, fire hall, schoolhouse and much more. The village holds many special activities and celebrations throughout the year. Call for more information.

Seasons/Hours: Memorial Day–Labor Day: 10 am–5 pm M–Sa; 1 pm–5 pm Su; or by appointment

Cost: Adults: $6, youth under 15: $1

Address: 501 Stower Dr, Worthington, MN 56187

Phone: 507.376.3125 or 507.376.4431

E-mail: nchs@frontiernet.net

Website: www.stenseth.org/hs/nobles.html

Directions: From I-90, take Exit 42 to Hwy 59 to Oxford St and turn right. Go to the stoplight and turn right. Watch for signs.

ROCK COUNTY HISTORICAL MUSEUM

84 Description: This museum is in the former Masonic Temple. Its exhibits include collections pertinent to the history of the county, and the Military Room filled with memorabilia dating as far back as the Civil War. Extensive newspaper and obituary files are part of the genealogical research sources available. The RCHS also maintains a century-old barn at the Rock County Fairgrounds, which holds agricultural artifacts and is open for special events.

Seasons/Hours: June–Aug: 2 pm–4 pmTu, Th & Sa

Address: 123 N Freeman Ave N, Luverne, MN

Phone: 507.283.2122

E-mail: info@LuverneMN.com

Website: www.luvernemn.com/historical_museum.htm

Directions: From Hwy 75 in Luverne, turn E one block on Main St to Luverne Ave and go one block N.

WELCOME HISTORICAL MUSEUM

85 Description: Volunteer guides will show how pioneers lived and worked, doing everyday tasks such as grinding coffee and getting water from the cistern pump. A 1930s kitchen is on display, complete with a cookstove, icebox, butter churn and more. History of Welcome School can also be relived; look at old uniforms and yearbooks, trophies and photos from 1908 to 1989.

Seasons/Hours: April–Sept: 2 pm–4 pm W & Sa

Cost: Free

Address: 109 Hulseman St, Welcome, MN 56181

Phone: 507.728.8617

Directions: From Fairmont, take I-90 W, exit to Hwy 263 and go S. Turn right on 2nd St W in Welcome, go to Hulseman St and turn left one block.

SOUTHWEST MINNESOTA FESTIVALS

LISTED ALPHABETICALLY

ALLIS CHALMERS
BIG ORANGE
SPECTACULAR

Description: This is the largest Allis Chalmers show in North America. There is plenty to see and do: tractors, implements, toys, memorabilia, demonstrations and a kids' pedal tractor pull.

Occurrence: July

Write to: Upper Midwest AC Club, 22241 200th St, Hutchinson, MN 55350

Phone: 320.587.3772 or 320.587.3771

E-mail: acclub@hutchtel.net

Directions: From Minneapolis, take Hwy 7 W to Hutchinson, then Hwy 15 S to 200th St, then go W.

CHRISTMAS IN
THE VILLAGE

Description: Bring the family to see the old-fashioned lighted village, Santa, children's crafts and lots of entertainment. Go on a sleigh ride, shop the craft and bake sales and stop at the candy store. There is a new theme annually.

Occurrence: First Saturday in December

Write to: 151 Pioneer Dr, PO Box 303, Montevideo, MN 56265

Phone: 320.269.7636

E-mail: cchs.june@juno.com

Directions: Located in Montevideo's Historic Chippewa City at the intersection of Hwy 7 and Hwy 59.

 **CIVIL WAR FESTIVAL**

Description:	The Pipestone Civil War Days is a celebration of our past in a beautiful historic setting. Scheduled activities for the weekend include both infantry and artillery maneuvers, an authentic re-enactment of a Civil War battle and numerous demonstrations of historic life.
Occurrence:	Every even numbered year in early August
Write to:	Pipestone CVB, Box 8, Pipestone, MN 56164
Phone:	507.825.3316
E-mail:	pipecham@pipestoneminnesota.com
Website:	www.pipestoneminnesota.com
Directions:	From the Twin Cities go S on I-35 to Owatonna, then W on Hwy 14 through Mankato. Take Hwy 23 S to Pipestone. Event is held in Pipestone City Limits

 **DANUBE FUN DAYS**

Description:	An ice cream social, parade, volleyball tournament and crafts in the park put the fun in Danube Fun Days.
Occurrence:	Second weekend in July
Write to:	City of Danube, PO Box 397, 400 2nd St, Danube, MN 56230-0397
Phone:	Contact Veva at 320.826.2563
E-mail:	danube@tds.net
Website:	www.cityofdanube.com, then click "events" then "Danube Fun Days"
Directions:	Danube is 100 mi. W of Minneapolis/St. Paul on Hwy 212.

 **INTERLAKEN HERITAGE DAYS**

Description:	Come out and see the Borderline Cruisers Car Show, a flea market, craft show, food vendors, on-stage entertainers, children's games, a carnival, and a parade.
Occurrence:	June
Write to:	Fairmont Chamber of Commerce, 206 N State St,

	PO Box 826, Fairmont, MN 56031
Phone/Fax:	Ph: 507.235.5547 or 800.657.3280; Fax: 507.235.8411
E-mail:	Kathy@fairmontcvb.com
Directions:	Take I-90 W to Hwy 15, then go S to Fairmont.

JACKSON RACE DAYS

Description:	Nothing says summer fun like a parade, sprint car races, a soap box derby, car and tractor shows, food and craft stands, beer and brats, sports tournaments and a dance.
Occurrence:	Third weekend in July
Write to:	82 W Ashley St, Jackson, MN 56143
Phone:	507.847.3867 or 507.847.4423
E-mail:	chamber@cityofjacksonmn.com
Directions:	Jackson is located at the intersection of Hwy 71 and I-90.

LITCHFIELD MEMORIAL DAY PICNIC

Description:	Eat hot dogs, BBQ sandwiches, beans and chips, and partake in an all-American picnic with the community.
Occurrence:	Memorial Day
Write to:	308 N Marshall Ave, Litchfield, MN 55355
Phone:	320.693.8911
E-mail:	webbie@hutchtel.net
Directions:	From the Twin Cities, take Hwy 12 W to Litchfield, exit right onto 3rd St and go E one block to Marshall.

LUVERNE BUFFALO DAYS

| *Description:* | This is a weekend packed with fun activities: a parade, arts in the park with over 130 vendors, entertainment and an auto show. Come for the uniqueness of Buffalo Days' namesake: the world-famous buffalo chip throwing contest and free buffalo burger feed. Activities held at the Luverne City Park. |
| *Occurrence:* | First weekend in June |

Write to:	Luverne Chamber of Commerce, 102 E Main St, Luverne, MN 56156
Phone/Fax:	Ph: 507.283.4061 or 888.283.4061; Fax: 507.283.4061
E-mail:	luvernechamber@iw.net
Website:	www.luvernemn.com/events/buffalo-days/default.asp
Directions:	From Minneapolis, S I 35 to W I 90. Right on US 75, right on Main St.

MARSHALL'S FESTIVAL OF TREES

Description:	See trees beautifully decorated on Main Street by Marshall businesses in the spirit of Christmas. Community members vote on the best tree, but you can be the judge.
Occurrence:	December
Write to:	115 W College Dr, Marshall, MN 56258
Phone:	507.537.8245
E-mail:	Deboer@schwans.com
Directions:	From Minneapolis, take Hwy 212 W to Granite Falls, then S on Hwy 23 to Marshall.

MONTEVIDEO FIESTA DAYS

Description:	Good times to be had by all: a parade, car show, chicken BBQ, canoe race, fishing contest, golf, softball and tennis tournaments, and much more. Most activities are on Main St and in Smith Park.
Occurrence:	Third weekend in June
Write to:	Montevideo Area Chamber of Commerce, 110 N 1st St, Suite 2, Montevideo, MN 56265
Phone:	800.269.5527 or (866) 866.5432
E-mail:	chamber@maxminn.com
Directions:	From Minneapolis, W on US 12, merge onto W MN 23, right onto MN 7 to Montevideo.

NEW ULM HERITAGEFEST

Description: Heritagefest® is a unique Old-World celebration. The whole family can enjoy the music of New Ulm's own Concord Singers and European musicians performing on five stages. Come inside to the air-conditioned Fest Halle and devour German food and beverages. It's all here—discover Germany in Minnesota.

Occurrence: Second and third weekends in July

Write to: PO Box 461, New Ulm, MN 56073

Phone: 507.354.8850

E-mail: hfest@newulmtel.net

Website: www.heritagefest.org

Directions: From the Twin Cities, go 90 mi. SW on Hwy 169 to St. Peter, then take Hwy 99 SW to Nicollet. Go on Hwy 14 W to New Ulm, Hwy 27 to Broadway, then N to 12th St N, W to State S to the Brown County Fairgrounds.

OKTOBERFEST

Description: Features musical entertainment, including the Concord Singers German food, a craft show and trolley rides on Saturday past New Ulm historic homes.

Occurrence: First two weekends in October

Write to: The Holiday Inn, 2101 S Broadway, New Ulm, MN 56073

Phone: 888.4NEWULM

E-mail: nuchamber@newulmtel.net

Directions: From Hwy 169, go to St. Peter and take Hwy 99 through Nicollet to Hwy 14 into New Ulm.

OLD GLORY DAYS

Description: Held at "Snyder Flats" at the Hole in the Mountain City Park, Old Glory Days hosts a day filled with music, crafts and food.

Occurrence: First Saturday in July

Write to: Lake Benton Chamber of Commerce, PO Box 205, Lake Benton, MN 56149

Phone:	507.368.9577
Directions:	Go S on I-35 to Owatonna, then W on Hwy 14 through Mankato to Lake Benton.

 **OLE AND LENA DAYS**

Description:	Get back to your Norwegian roots with a sense of humor in this heritage celebration consisting of entertainment, a snow sculpturing contest, Uff Da Bargain Days, a medallion hunt, a road race, sleigh rides, a craft show and a dance and much more.
Occurrence:	January
Write to:	Granite Falls Chamber of Commerce, 155 7th Ave, PO Box 220, Granite Falls, MN 56241
Phone/Fax:	Ph: 320.564.4039; Fax: 320.564.3210
E-mail:	gfchamber@kilowatt.net
Website:	www.granitefalls.com/pages/calendar.htm
Directions:	From the Twin Cities, go W on Hwy 212 to Granite Falls.

 **ORTONVILLE CORN FEST**

Description:	Activities include the Ortonville Area Queen Pageant, Big Stone Cruisers Car Show, arts and crafts, 5K and 10K races, kids' games and a pedal tractor pull. Sink your teeth into a free sweet corn feed, a parade, fireworks, an airshow and the Fly-In Breakfast. With new attractions every year, there is something fun for everyone.
Occurrence:	Third weekend in August
Write to:	41 NW 2nd St, Ortonville, MN 56278
Phone/Fax:	Ph: 320.839.3284 or 800.568.5722; Fax: 320.839.2621
E-mail:	chamber@bigstonelake.com
Website:	www.bigstonelake.com
Directions:	Ortonville is at the intersection of Hwy 12 and Hwy 75.

PIONEER POWER
SWAP MEET

Description:	With over 1,000 antique machines, farm collectibles, and flea market vendors, this is largest event of its type in the United States.
Occurrence:	Late April
Write to:	27548 376th St, Le Sueur, MN 56058
Phone:	507.665.2868 or 952.758.4926
E-mail:	dbriebel@prairie.lakes.com
Directions:	From Hwy 169, exit on Hwy 93 through Le Sueur. Go E on Hwy 26 six mi. out of town to the Le Sueur County Pioneer Association Showgrounds.

POLSKA KIELBASA
DAYS

Description:	This is a celebration of the town's Polish heritage. Join in golf, softball, volleyball, and basketball tournaments, a tractor pull competition, karaoke and square dancing. Top off this event with its signature kielbasa (Polish sausage) for lunch or dinner.
Occurrence:	Second weekend in August
Write to:	PO Box 54, Ivanhoe, MN 56142
Phone:	507.694.1246
E-mail:	cityivan@frontiernet.net
Directions:	From Minneapolis take Hwy 212 W to Hwy 75 S, to Cty Rd 18 E to Ivanhoe.

RAILROAD DAYS

Description:	Get into the spirit of this small-town summer festival. There is a four-mile rail run and walk, pedal pull, crafts, an antique and flea market, ball tournaments, trolley rides, a dance and parade.
	The roundhouse is open free to the public during "Railroad Days" and features model railroad layouts in HO, O(Lionel) and G scale.
Occurrence:	June
Write to:	St. James Area Chamber of Commerce, 514 2nd Ave S, PO Box 346, St. James, MN 56081-0346

Phone/Fax:	Ph: 507.375.3333 or (866) 375.2480; Fax: 507.375.3334
Website:	www.stjamesmn.org, click on "Community Events" then click on "Railroad Days"
Directions:	From the Twin Cities, go S on I-35 to US Hwy 14. Go W to Mankato, then get on Hwy 60 which will turn into Hwy 15 at Madelia, then turns into Hwy 30 at St. James.

SHARE OUR HERITAGE INDIAN ARTS FESTIVAL

Description:	This event focuses on showcasing the culture of the American Indian people as well as the pioneers in order to share the heritage of these early American peoples. Through music, food, dance, and hands-on arts and crafts presentations, visitors can catch a glimpse of what was happening in the Pipestone area during an earlier era.
	This festival is organized by the Keeper's Gift Shop Gallery, offering supplies for arts and crafts, seminars on the history of the depot and the railroad that ran through Pipestone, as well as different styles of peacepipes. It also holds workshops giving instruction on beadwork, pipes and leatherwork.
Occurrence:	Late July or early August, call for specific dates
Write to:	400 N Hiawatha Ave, PO Box 24, Pipestone, MN 56164 or Pipestone CVB, Box 8, Pipestone, MN 56164
Phone:	507.825.3734; CVB: 507.825.3316
E-mail:	pipecham@pipestoneminnesota.com
Directions:	From Mankato, take Hwy 14 W to Florence, then Hwy 23 S to Pipestone. Take a right on Hwy 75 then an immediate left onto 4th St. Go over the railroad tracks to the stop sign, and go right onto Hiawatha Ave to the old depot. Look for the 28-foot peace pipe sculpture in front. The festival takes place in the park N of the depot.

UPPER SIOUX COMMUNITY TRADITIONAL WACIPI

Description:	Celebrate with the Upper Sioux Community in song, dance and drumming. This event is held at the Upper Sioux Agency State Park Travel Center.
Occurrence:	August
Write to:	Granite Falls Chamber of Commerce, 155 7th Ave, PO Box 220, Granite Falls, MN 56241
Phone/Fax:	Ph: 320.564.4039; Fax: 320.564.3210

E-mail:	pwaters@info-link.net
Directions:	From the Twin Cities, go W on Hwy 212 to Granite Falls.

WANDA GAG CHRISTMAS

Description:	Join in the creation of two Christmas trees based on Wanda Gag's books. See two beautifully decorated trees that would have made Wanda Gag's dreams come true.
Occurrence:	December
Write to:	226 N Washington, Box 432, New Ulm, MN 56073
Phone:	507.359.2632 or 507.354.8081
Directions:	From Hwy 169, go to St. Peter and take Hwy 99 through Nicollet to Hwy 14 into New Ulm. Take a left, still Hwy 14 to the first stoplight and turn right to the 3rd N. Between 2nd and 3rd watch for a sign, take a left and come up two blocks.

WORTHINGTON INTERNATIONAL FESTIVAL

Description:	Venture around the world without leaving Worthington. There are arts, children's activities, a talent show, music and sports of Mexico, Africa, Asia, and Europe (including a soccer tournament). Taste ethnic food while listening to gospel and rhythmic music.
Occurrence:	July
Write to:	Worthington CVB, 1121 3rd Ave, Worthington, MN 56187
Phone:	507.372.2919 or 507.372.8210
E-mail:	dmackl@frontiernet.net
Directions:	From the Twin Cities, take I-35 S to I-90. Go W into Worthington. Go S on US Hwy 51, which becomes Humiston Ave, to 14th St. Go E to 1st Ave three blocks to 11th Ave, then N two blocks.

COUNTIES INCLUDED IN THIS SECTION:

BIG STONE COUNTY was established in 1862. It was named for the outcropping of granite and gneiss that can be found at Big Stone Lake. The county seat is Ortonville. The area 528 square miles, which ranks 67th in the state. Population is 5,820 people, which ranks 1st in Minnesota. Population density is 11.7 people per square mile, which ranks 71st in the state.

BLUE EARTH COUNTY was established in 1853. It was named for the blue-green clay which can be found in the area. The county seat is Mankato. The area is 766 square miles, which ranks 32nd in the state. Population is 55,941 people, which ranks 15th in Minnesota. Population density is 74.4 people per square mile, which ranks 17th in the state.

BROWN COUNTY was established in 1855. It was named for Joseph R. Brown, a prominent settler, soldier, drummer boy, politician, trader, and editor, among other occupations. The county seat is New Ulm. The area is 619 square miles, which ranks 52nd in the state. Population is 2,6911 people, which ranks 37th in Minnesota. Population density is 44.1 people per square mile, which ranks 30th in the state.

CHIPPEWA COUNTY was established in 1862. It was named for the Chippewa Indians who were known to make use of the river, which now bears their name as a war road. The county seat is Montevideo. The area is 588 square miles, which ranks 56th in the state. Population is 13,088 people,which ranks 62nd in Minnesota. Population density is 22.5 people per square mile, which ranks 51st in the state.

COTTONWOOD COUNTY was established in 1857. It was named for the Cottonwood River which flows through the county. The river was named for the abundance of cottonwood trees along its banks. The county seat is Windom. The area is 649 square miles, which ranks 9th in the state. Population is 12,167 people, which ranks 63rd in Minnesota. Population density is 19 people per square mile, which ranks 57th in the state.

FARIBAULT COUNTY was established in 1855. It was named for Jean Baptiste Faribault, a trader who dealt with the Dakota. The county seat is Blue Earth. The area is 722 square miles, which ranks 39th in the state. Population is 16,181 people, which ranks 55th in Minnesota. Population density is 22.7 people per square mile, which ranks 50th in the state.

JACKSON COUNTY was established in 1857. It was named for Henry Jackson who was the first merchant in St. Paul. He was also a member of the first territorial legislature. The county seat is Jackson. The area is 719 square miles, which ranks 43rd in the state. Population 11,268 people, which ranks 66th in Minnesota. Population density is 16.1 people per square mile, which ranks 63rd in the state.

KANDIYOHI COUNTY was established in 1858. It was named after the Native American word meaning "where the buffalo fish come." The county seat is Willmar. The area 862 square miles, which ranks 29th in the state. Population is 41,203 people, which ranks 1st in Minnesota. Population density is 51.8 people per square mile, which ranks 25th in the state.

LAC QUI PARLE COUNTY was established in 1871. It was named for the French word meaning "lake that speaks." The county seat is Madison. The area is 788 square miles, which ranks 31st in the state. Population is 8,067 people, which ranks 76th in Minnesota. Population density is 10.5 people per square mile, which ranks 73rd in the state.

LE SUEUR COUNTY was established in 1853. It was named for the French explorer Pierre Charles Le Sueur who traveled along what is now known as the Minnesota River in 1770. The county seat is Le Center. The area is 474 square miles, which ranks 71st in the state. Population is 25,426 people, which ranks 39th in Minnesota. Population density is 56.7 people per square mile, which ranks 22nd in the state.

LINCOLN COUNTY was established in 1873. After three failed attempts to honor President Abraham Lincoln, this county was finally named after him. The county seat is Ivanhoe. The area is 548 square miles, which ranks 64th in the state. Population is 6,429 people, which ranks 79th in Minnesota. Population density is 12 people per square mile, which ranks 70th in the state.

LYON COUNTY was established in 1868. It was named for General Nathaniel Lyon who served in the Union Army during the Civil War and was killed in 1861. The county seat is Marshall. The area is 721 square miles, which ranks 40th in the state. Population is 25,425 people, which ranks 40th in Minnesota. Population density is 35.6 people per square mile, which ranks 36th in the state.

MARTIN COUNTY was established in 1857. It was named for either Henry Martin who owned many acres in the area, or Morgan Lewis Martin who was a congressional delegate from the Wisconsin Territory. The county seat is Fairmont. The area is 730 square miles, which ranks 36th in the state. Population is 21,802 people, which ranks 44th in Minnesota. Population density is 30.7 people per square mile, which ranks 39th in the state.

MCLEOD COUNTY was established in 1856. It was named for Martin McLeod who was a fur trader and later president of the territorial council. The county seat is Glencoe. The area 506 square miles, which ranks 69th in the state. Population is 34,898 people, which ranks 25th in Minnesota. Population density is 70.9 people per square mile, which ranks 19th in the state.

MEEKER COUNTY was established in 1856. It was named for Bradley Meeker who was a justice of the territorial court from 1849-1853. The county seat is Litchfield. The area is 645 square miles, which ranks 50th in the state. Population is 22,644 people, which ranks 42nd in Minnesota. Population density is 37.2 people per square mile, which ranks 34th in the state.

MURRAY COUNTY was established in 1857. It was named for William P. Murray, a lawyer who was also a member of the state constitutional convention and later served as a senator. The county seat is Slayton. The area is 720 square miles, which ranks 42nd in the state. Population is 9,165 people, which ranks 74th in Minnesota. Population density is 13 people per square mile, which ranks 69th in the state.

NICOLLET COUNTY was established in 1853. Named for Joseph Nicollet, a cartographer who made the first accurate map of the area. The county seat is St. Peter. The area is 467 square miles, which ranks 72nd in the state. Population is 29,771 people, which ranks 35th in Minnesota. Population density is 65.8 people per square mile, which ranks 20th in the state.

NOBLES COUNTY was established in 1857. It was named for William Nobles who was member of the territorial legislature in 1854 and 1856. The county seat is Worthington. The area is 722 square miles, which ranks 38th in the state. Population is 20,832 people, which ranks 47th in Minnesota. Population density is 29.1 people per square mile, which ranks 40th in the state.

PIPESTONE COUNTY was established in 1857. It was named for the red pipestone found in the area by the Native Americans who used it for pipe bowls. The county seat is Pipestone. The area is 466 square miles, which ranks 73rd in the state. Population is 9,895 people, which ranks 72nd in Minnesota. Population density is 21.2 people per square mile, which ranks 53rd in the state.

REDWOOD COUNTY was established in 1862. The Dakota named this area for its abundance of red willow trees. The county seat is Redwood Falls. The area is 881 square miles, which ranks 25th in the state. Population is 16,815 people, which ranks 53rd in Minnesota. Population density is 19.1 people per square mile, which ranks 56th in the state.

RENVILLE COUNTY was established in 1855. It was named for Joseph Renville, an explorer, trader and interpreter during the War of 1812. The county seat is Olivia. The area is 987 square miles, which ranks 23rd in the state. Population is 17,154 people, which ranks 52nd in Minnesota. Population density is 17.5 people per square mile, which ranks 60th in the state.

ROCK COUNTY was established in 1857. It was named for a prominent rock outcropping rising about 175 feet above the prairie, often referred to as "The Mound." The county seat is Luverne. The area is 483 square miles, which ranks 70th in the state. Population is 9,721 people, which ranks 73rd in Minnesota. Population density is 20.1 people per square mile, which ranks 54th in the state.

SIBLEY COUNTY was established in 1853. It was named for General Henry Hastings Sibley, the first governor of Minnesota. The county seat is Gaylord. The area is 600 square miles, which ranks 55th in the state. Population is 15,356 people, which ranks 56th in Minnesota. Population density is 26.1 people per square mile, which ranks 45th in the state.

SWIFT COUNTY was established in 1870. It was named for Henry Adoniram Swift who was governor in 1863. The county seat is Benson. The area is 752 square miles, which ranks 34th in the state. Population is 11,956 people, which ranks 64th in Minnesota. Population density is 16.1 people per square mile, which ranks 64th in the state.

WASECA COUNTY was established in 1857. It was named for the Dakota word meaning "fertile" or "rich." The county seat Waseca. The area is 433 square miles, which ranks 80th in the state. Population is 19,526 people, which ranks 49th in Minnesota. Population density is 46.1 people per square mile, which ranks 28th in the state.

WATONWAN COUNTY was established in 1860. The word may have been a mis-translation of the Dakota language; its modern-day name means "I see" but the intended name, "Watonwan," means "fish bait." The county seat is St. James. The area is 440 square miles, which ranks 78th in the state. Population is 11,876 people, which ranks 65th in Minnesota. Population density is 27.3 people per square mile, which ranks 44th in the state.

YELLOW MEDICINE COUNTY was established in 1872. Yellow Medicine River and Yellow Medicine County were named after a moonseed plant—"Pejihutazizi"—Dakota for "yellow medicine." The county seat is Granite Falls. The area is 763 square miles, which ranks 33rd in the state. Population is 11,080 people, which ranks 68th in Minnesota. Population density is 14.6 people per square mile, which ranks 67th in the state.

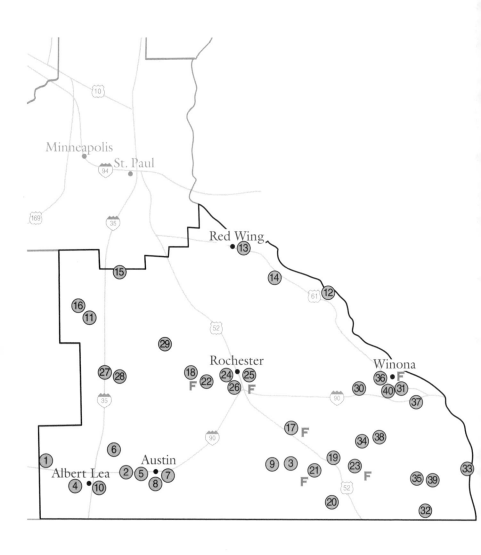

SOUTHEAST MINNESOTA

ATTRACTIONS WITHIN AN HOUR'S DRIVE OF:

(#) = historic sites   **F** = festivals

Listings in grey print are found in other sections but are within an hour's drive of the city.

See Metro Section for additional sites within an hours drive of this city

ALDEN MUSEUM

(1) *Description:*   Home to three stories of history, this museum is chock-full of antiques, farming equipment and genealogical resources. One room has been restored to twentieth century living quarters, and another room holds miscellaneous items in an old-time store setting.

Seasons/Hours: Memorial Day–Labor Day: 10 am–2 pm F; or by appointment 507.874.3317

Cost: Donations accepted

Address: 115 N Broadway, PO Box 486, Alden, MN 56009

Phone: 507.874.3462

Website: www.freeborncounty.com/alden.htm

Directions: Take Exit 146 off of I-90 then turn N to Broadway.

CZECH BRICK HALL

(2) *Description:*   This building is on the National Historic Register. There are old photographs and a hand-painted stage screen.

Seasons/Hours: Call for appointment

Address: Hayward, MN 56043

Phone: 507.373.2673

Directions: From Myrtle, go ½ mi. N on Cty Rd 30.

ED'S MUSEUM AND LIVING QUARTERS

(3) *Description:*   For his last 50 years, Ed Krueger, while owning and operating a Jack Sprat Food Store, accumulated many treasures. After his death in 1989, the building willed to the city, the Wykoff Area Historical Society was formed and his dream of it becoming a museum came true. The museum is jam-packed with all of Ed's memorabilia, including his pet cat, player piano and every issue of *Life* magazine from 1938–1972.

Seasons/Hours: June–Sept: 1 pm–4 pm Sa–Su; or by appointment

Cost: Free, donations accepted

Address: 100 S Gold St, Wykoff, MN 55990

Website: www.dwave.net/~schnabl/wykoffMN.htm#attractions

Directions:	From Rochester, go 35 mi. SE on Hwy 16. Turn N on Hwy 80 into Wykoff. Museum is across from Security State Bank.

FREEBORN COUNTY HISTORICAL SOCIETY MUSEUM, LIBRARY & HISTORICAL VILLAGE

④ *Description:*	The museum's main building includes a library, genealogical and area history research office. There is an exhibit area that includes a kitchen and living room. Examples of a toy shop, doctor, dentist and printing office are on display as well as collections of musical instruments, dolls and pioneer living. The village extends beyond the museum with 18 additional buildings.
Seasons/Hours:	Year-round museum and library: 10 am–5 pm Tu–F; May–Sept: museum and village: 10 am–5 pm Tu–F; 1 pm–5 pm Sa; closed holidays; tours by appointment
Cost:	Adults: $5, youth ages 12–18: $1
Address:	1031 Bridge Ave, Albert Lea, MN 56007
Phone:	507.373.8003
E-mail:	bjackso@smig.net or fchm@smig.net
Website:	www.smig.net/fchm
Directions:	Located two mi. S of I-90 next to fairgrounds at Hawthorne St and Bridge Ave intersection.
Don't miss this:	The Freeborn County Historical Society has a brochure available to guide visitors through a walking tour of Albert Lea. There are 27 sites listed on the tour, of which four are on the National Register of Historic Places. The tour guide is available in the Albert Lea visitor's guide. Starting at Broadway and Clark St, check out over 20 buildings that were built between 1874 and 1923.

GREIBROKS MINI HISTORY FARM AND COUNTY FAIR

⑤ *Description:*	There are 34 rooms with over 700 toys, tractors, old farm equipment, cars, dolls, an Africa Room and even some carnival rides.
Seasons/Hours:	Year-round: 8 am–8 pm daily; or by appointment
Cost:	Free, donations appreciated
Address:	16821 890 Ave, Oakland, MN
Phone:	507.433.4880

Website:	www.koa.com/where/morekampgroundinfo/ 23101attractions.htm
Directions:	From Austin, go 3½ mi. W, then 5 mi. S on Cty Rd 34.

HOLLANDALE HERITAGE HUIS

⑥ *Description:*	This is a one-room museum filled with artifacts from Hollandale and the surrounding area.
Seasons/Hours:	Open by appointment
Address:	Box 184, Hollandale, MN 56045
Phone:	507.889.3017
Directions:	From I-35, take the Clarks Grove Exit and go six mi. E. Located on Main St in Hollandale.

MOWER COUNTY HISTORICAL CENTER

⑦ *Description:*	Home to over ten museums, tons of historical records, and a visitor store, this site has it all. Included are a log cabin museum, rural school museum, railroad museum with a steam locomotive and caboose, firemen's museum, blacksmith shop and many more. Meander through the fairgrounds as the town itself once existed. Then you can browse plat books, newspapers and other census records, some of which date back as far as the 1860s.
Seasons/Hours:	Year-round: 10 am–4 pm M–F
Cost:	Adults: $5, students: $1, children under 10: free with an adult
Address:	1303 6th Ave SW, PO Box 804, Austin, MN 55912
Phone:	507.437.6082
E-mail:	mchs@smig.net
Website:	www2.smig.net/mchistory/
Directions:	Located at the Mower County Fairgrounds in Austin.

⑧ Description: Spam history, Spam trivia, Spam around the world, even a Spam short film, you'll find all this and more at the Spam Museum in its hometown of Austin. With its many interactive exhibits, this museum is an educational and fun field trip experience for children of all ages. And for that hard-to-shop-for loved one check out the Spam store for everything from pencils to boxers.

Seasons/Hours: May 1–Labor Day: 10 am–5 pm M–Sa; 12 pm–4 pm Su; Labor Day–April 31: 10 am–5 pm Tu–Sa; 12 pm–4 pm Su

Cost: Free

Address: 1937 Spam Blvd, Austin, MN 55912

Phone: 800.LUV.SPAM (800.588.7726)

E-mail: slradford@hormel.com

Website: www.spam.com

Directions: Take Exit 178B off I-90 in Austin.

Spam Museum

SPRING VALLEY METHODIST CHURCH MUSEUM

⑨ Description: This 1876 Methodist Church Museum is where the James Wilder family were members. James's son, Almanzo, and Laura (Ingalls) Wilder attended this church in 1890 and 1891. See a photo display of the Wilder family and an exhibit depicting the life of Richard Sears, the co-founder of the Sears & Roebuck Catalog Company, who lived and went to school in Spring Valley for nine years. An 1874 wooden fire wagon and much more is on display.

Seasons/Hours:	Memorial Day–Labor Day: 10 am–4 pm daily; Sept & Oct: 10 am–4 pm Sa & Su
Cost:	Adults: $3, students: $1
Address:	221 W Courtland, Spring Valley, MN 55975
Phone:	507.346.7659
Directions:	One block W of downtown business district in Spring Valley.

STORY LADY DOLL AND TOY MUSEUM

⑩ *Description:*	There are over 1,500 dolls and toys on exhibit in the museum. The collection features dolls from classic story books such as Pinocchio, Cinderella and Snow White, as well as contemporary literature such as Madeline, Strega Nona, Pooh Bear and others. There are also antique German and French dolls, china heads, a collection of ethnic dolls and handcarved dancing dolls. The museum offers birthday parties at which children are able to dress up in party clothes and hats. A gift shop is open to the public.
Seasons/Hours:	Year-round: 12 pm–4 pm Tu–F; 11 am–3 pm Sa; group tours are available by appointment
Cost:	Adults: $2, children 12 and under: $1
Address:	131 N Broadway, Albert Lea, MN 56007
Phone:	507.377.1820
Website:	www.albertleatourism.org/storylady.htm
Directions:	From Main St, then go N on Broadway. The museum and gift shop are located in downtown Albert Lea.

ALEXANDER FARIBAULT HOUSE

⑪ *Description:*	In 1826 Alexander Faribault came to the area to trade with the Wapakhute Indians, and the area has never been the same. His home, which dates back to 1853, was the first frame-style house built in the county. The site is open to visitors and can accommodate groups of 45 or more.
Seasons/Hours:	April 1–Oct 1: 1 pm–4 pm M–F; other times by appointment
Cost:	Adults: $2, children: $1; RCHS members: free
Address:	12 1st Ave NE, Faribault, MN 55021
Phone:	507.334.7913 or 507.332.2121
Directions:	Located in downtown Faribault.

ARROWHEAD BLUFFS MUSEUM

⑫ **Description:** This museum is home to every Winchester gun model produced between 1866 and 1982. You will also find an impressive collection of Native American artifacts and many mounted animals throughout the museum.

Seasons/Hours: Apr–Dec: 10 am–6 pm daily

Cost: Adults: $4; students ages 12–18: $3; children ages 6–11: $2; groups by appointment: $3; group bus drivers: free

Address: Rt 3, Box 7, Wabasha, MN 55981

Phone: 651.565.3829

Directions: Located two mi. W of Wabasha on Hwy 60.

GOODHUE COUNTY HISTORICAL SOCIETY AND MUSEUM

⑬ **Description:** The Goodhue County Historical Society is among the oldest historical societies in Minnesota. Their museum has exhibits specializing in area geology, Native American history (especially the Dakota Indians), military, natural history, sports and agriculture. Red Wing Pottery is also on display, and its library has research materials available to the public. School tours and educational programs are offered to people of all ages.

Seasons/Hours: Year-round: 10 am–5 pm Tu–F; 1 pm–5 pm Sa–Su; closed holidays

Cost: Adults: $5, seniors: $3, children: free

Address: 1166 Oak St, Red Wing, MN 55066

Phone/Fax: Ph: 651.388.6024; Fax: 651.388.3577

E-mail: goodhuecountyhis@qwest.net

Website: www.goodhuehistory.mus.mn.us

Directions: From the N on Hwy 61 in Red Wing, turn right onto West Ave and go five blocks. Turn right on College Ave which curves to the right at the top of the hill onto Oak St. The museum is at the end of Oak St.

From the S on Hwy 61, turn left onto Bush St and go five blocks. Turn right onto 7th St. At the 5-way intersection go straight up College Ave which curves to the right at the top of the hill onto Oak St. The museum is at the end of Oak St.

James Goodhue published the first issue of the *Minnesota Pioneer* in 1849.

LAKE CITY HISTORIC WALKING TOUR

(14) Description: Lake City is located on Lake Pepin, which is part of the Mississippi River. This walking tour takes visitors past 15 historic buildings and sites in the city. Pick up detailed brochures at the area Chamber of Commerce.

Write to: Lake City Area Chamber of Commerce, 212 S Washington St, PO Box 150, Lake City, MN 55041

Phone: 800.369.4123

E-mail: lcchamber@earthlink.net

Website: www.lakecitymn.org/attractions.html, the click on "Historic District"

Directions: From Hwy 61, go one block W on Washington St to Chamber of Commerce building to pick up a map.

NORTHFIELD HISTORICAL SOCIETY BANK MUSEUM

(15) Description: In 1876 Jesse James and his gang raided the Northfield Bank. The Northfield Historical Society has restored the bank to its condition in 1876. There is an interpretive center that tells about the raid and displays artifacts from the gang. In September there is an annual re-enactment of the raid.

Seasons/Hours: Year-round: 10 am–4 pm daily; or by appointment

Cost: Adults: $4, children: $1.50

Address: 408 Division St, Northfield, MN 55057

Phone: 507.645.9268

E-mail: nhsmuseum@rconnect.com

Website: www.northfieldhistory.org/NHS/site.html

Directions: Located in downtown Northfield.

In 1876 after the James gang tried to rob the Northfield Bank, they were pursued by a large posse and then cornered in a marsh north of Madelia. Frank and Jesse escaped but the Younger brothers were captured.

RICE COUNTY HISTORICAL SOCIETY

⑯ Description: This museum houses everything from prehistoric artifacts to present-day collectibles. In addition to its many exhibits, there are also many restored buildings, a video and a genealogical center. Guided tours are available.

Seasons/Hours: Year-round: 9 am–4 pm M–F; summer hours: 1 pm–4 pm Sa–Su

Cost: Adults: $3, seniors: $2, children 13 and under: $1; RCHS members: free

Address: 1814 2nd Ave NW, Faribault, MN 55021

Phone: 507.332.2121

Directions: Take I-35 S to Hwy 21 S, then to Hwy 3. Take a right on 2nd Ave NW and go down two blocks.

CHATFIELD HISTORICAL SOCIETY AND PEASE MUSEUM

⑰ Description: Though small in space, this museum is packed with artifacts about the area. Information about area artists, the Chatfield area residents and the railroad can be found here. Items in the museum have tags attached with the names of families who donated. See the taxidermy collection of outdoorsman William Pease, and learn details of Chatfield banker George Haven—two prominent figures from the area.

Seasons/Hours: Oct–May: 10 am–2 pm 1st Tu of month; or by appointment

Address: 21 2nd St SE, Chatfield, MN 55923

Phone: City Hall: 507.867.3810

Directions: From Rochester, S on Hwy 52 towards Preston. In Chatfield, go left on 2nd St near the Olmsted Medical Center. The museum is on the lower level of the first brick building on the left side.

Don't miss this: Two blocks from this museum is the Veterans' Memorial Museum in Chatfield, which houses WWI, WWII and Civil War artifacts. The Veterans' Museum, 314 Main Street, is open the 2nd Tu of month, 10 am–2 pm

DODGE COUNTY HISTORICAL SOCIETY

(18) Description: The Dodge County Historical Society is located in the former St. John's Episcopal Church which is made of local limestone. Much of the museum is filled with historic memorabilia and research material of Dodge County. Because of the county's well preserved architectural heritage, they have been included in the National Register Historical Places list.

Seasons/Hours: May 1–Oct 15: 10 am–4 pm Tu–Sa; Oct 16–April 31: 10 am–4 pm Th–Sa; closed Christmas and New Years

Cost: Adults: $2, seniors: $1.50; members and children under 12: free; contact the museum for group rates

Address: 615 N Main St, Mantorville, MN 55955-0433

Phone: 507.635.5508

E-mail: dchgc@tmtel.com

Website: www.dodgecohistorical.addr.com

Directions: From Rochester, take Hwy14 W to Hwy 57, go N on 57, take a left on 7th St. Mantorville Museum is on the left.

FILLMORE COUNTY HISTORICAL CENTER AND LIBRARY

(19) Description: The historical center has a collection of vintage tractors, tools, toys and Native American artifacts, plus rooms depicting different settings of time in the history of the county. There is a newspaper office, post office, country kitchen, a country school and a building that displays various agricultural equipment. The museum also has a large collection of vintage clothing including wedding dresses, fur accessories and hair wreaths. The museum is home to a 1932 Model T Sky Scout plane.

Seasons/Hours: Mid-Oct–mid-June: 9 am–4 pm M–F; mid-June–mid-Oct: 9 am–4 pm M–F; 1 pm–4:30 Sa–Su; closed holidays

Cost: Free

Address: 202 Cty Rd 8, Fountain, MN 55935

Phone/Fax: Ph: 507.268.4449; Fax: 507.268.4492

E-mail: fillmorehistory@earthlink.net

Directions: From Rochester head S on Hwy 53 to Cty Rd 8 in Fountain.

HARMONY TOY MUSEUM

(20) **Description:** The Harmony Toy Museum is the place to stop to see antique toys and small items. This museum offers a nostalgic look at the past; it contains over 4,000 items, including antique toys, pictures and prints. Other displays include trains, cars, dolls, and toy animals of many kinds.

Seasons/Hours: Year-round: 9 am–5 pm M–Sa; 12 pm–5 pm Su

Cost: Donation

Address: 30 Main Ave S, Harmony, MN 55939

Phone: 507.867.3380

Directions: From Rochester go S on Hwy 52 through Harmony. Turn right onto Main Ave and the Toy Museum is on the left side.

Don't miss this: While in Harmony check out the Amish tours or walking tours. Guides are available at the Information Center in Harmony.

HISTORIC FORESTVILLE

(21) **Description:** Within Forestville State Park, a living history program gives visitors a chance to see what the town was like for the families and workers in 1899. There are several stations including the store, house, garden, granary, carriage barn, and barn and cornfield, where costumed interpreters talk about their lives and provide the visitors with facts that will give them a better understanding of life in those days.

Minnesota Historical Society

Historic Forestville

Seasons/Hours: Memorial Day–Labor Day: 10 am–5 pm F; 11 am–6 pm Sa; 12 pm–5 pm Su; 10 am–5 pm M holidays; Sept–Oct: 10 am–5 pm Sa; 12 pm–5 pm Su

Cost: Adults: $4, children 6-12: $2; seniors and scheduled groups: $3; children under 6 and MHS members: free

Address: Rt 2, Box 128, Forestville State Park, Preston, MN 55965

Phone:	507.765.2785
E-mail:	forestville@mnhs.org
Website:	www.mnhs.org/places/sites/hf/index.html
Directions:	Located in Forestville State Park on Hwy 16 between Preston and Spring Valley; 30 mi. S of Rochester.

HISTORIC MANTORVILLE

㉒ *Description:*	The Mantorville Restoration House was used as the County Office buildings for the sheriff, register of deeds, and treasurer. Dodge County has one prison cell which was in the basement of the Restoration House.
	Take a tour through the 12 blocks of downtown Mantorville, listed on the National Register of Historic Places. Copies of the walking tour are available at the information center at the Riverside Mercantile. The map can be downloaded from www.mantorville.com/tour.html.
	There are 21 sites that will give more historical information about Mantorville, including the following: the Riverside Mercantile built in 1856, the 1860 Stone Barn Carriage House which was built from native limestone, a covered bridge and Goat Island, 1889 Grand Old Mansion, St Margaret's Catholic Church which was built in 1862, the 1871 Dodge County Court House that is one of the oldest buildings in the state that is in continual use, the 1918 Mantorville Opera House, among many others.
Seasons/Hours:	May–Oct: 12 pm–5 pm Tu–Su
Cost:	Donation
Address:	Mantorville, MN 55955
Phone:	507.635.5140
Website:	www.mantorville.com
Directions:	From Hwy 52, take Hwy 14 to Kasson, then N on Hwy 57 to Mantorville.

LANESBORO HISTORIC PRESERVATION ASSOCIATION AND MUSEUM

㉓ *Description:*	Historic Lanesboro is nestled in the beautiful Root River Valley. The Lanesboro Historic Preservation Association has paid close attention to keeping and showcasing the rich historical tradition of the Lanesboro area. The museum's collection includes a 100-

year-old spinning wheel and a locally donated doll collection, as well as other articles donated by local families.

A. Renee Bernstrom

Seasons/Hours: Call Info Center for hours

Cost: Free

Address: 105 Parkway S, Lanesboro, MN 55949

Phone: 507.467.2177; Info Center: 507.467.2696 or 800.944.2630

Website: www.lanesboro.com

Directions: From Rochester take Hwy 52 S to Fountain, then go E on Hwy 8 to Lanesboro. Turn right on Parkway S and museum is two doors down on the right.

Lanesboro Historic Museum

Don't miss this: This village was home to many prominent people who played a significant role in their community. The Lanesboro Heritage Preservation Commission has compiled a brochure for a self-guided walking tour through the residential area of Historic Lanesboro.

MAYOWOOD MANSION

㉔ Description: For three generations the Mayo family called this place their home. Now you can step back into the famous doctors' lives during the hour-long guided tour of the Mayowood estate. Be sure to visit during November when they host Christmas at the Mayowood Mansion.

Seasons/Hours: Seasonal tours May–Oct and Christmas tours in Nov. Call for schedule.

Cost: Adults: $10, children under 15: $5

Address: Mayowood Rd SW, Rochester, MN 55902

Phone: 507.282.9447

Website: www.olmstedhistory.com/mayowood.htm

Directions: From Hwy 52 in Rochester, go W on Cty Rd 125 (Mayowood Rd.) to the estate.

OLMSTED COUNTY HISTORICAL SOCIETY MUSEUM

㉕ Description: With exhibits spanning across the life of the county, this museum has a lot to offer. The hands-on cabin for children features many interactive exhibits, and the gift store with a used book section is worth checking out. The museum also has displays in both the William Dee Log Cabin and the George Stoppel Farm.

Seasons/Hours: Year-round: 9 am–5 pm Tu–Sa

Cost: Adults: $4, children: $1; OCHS members: free

Address: 1195 W Circle Dr SW., Rochester, MN 55902

Phone: 507.282.9447

E-mail: ochs@olmstedhistory.com

Website: www.olmstedhistory.com

Directions: Look for the covered wagon in front of the building on the corner of Hwy 22 and Hwy 25 SW, about two mi. W of the Apache Mall.

TRIVIA During the 1860s, the Rochester area had a three-day gold rush.

PLUMMER HOUSE

㉖ Description: Dr. Plummer organized, designed and worked at the Mayo clinic until the day he died in 1936. His former estate is home to 11 acres, 49 rooms, five fireplaces, a water tower and two caves. Visitors to the house will enjoy the original furniture and artifacts as well as the many gardens and trails to be found outdoors.

Seasons/Hours: June–Aug: 1 pm–5 pm W, 1st & 3rd Su of every month. The grounds are open from dawn to dusk.

Cost: Adults: $3, children 5-17: $1, children under 5: free

Address: 1091 Plummer Ln. SW, Rochester, MN 55902

Phone: 507.281.6160

Website: www.ci.rochester.mn.us/park/plummer/plummer.htm

Directions: From Hwy 52, take the 2nd St Exit, left at the stoplight and over the bridge to 14th Ave. Turn right, then take a left on 9th, then a right on Plummer Crl., and right at the Plummer House.

From downtown Rochester, take 2nd St to 14th Ave SW.

STATE SCHOOL ORPHANAGE MUSEUM

㉗ **Description:** From 1886–1945 the State Orphanage housed 10,635 children in its 16 on-site cottages. Buildings included a nursery, hospital, school, gymnasium, laundry, and superintendent and employee residences. The school also had its own power plant, greenhouse, icehouse, cemetery, and complete farm operation, making the institution self-sufficient. One can relive this unique chapter of American history through a self-guided tour. Videos are also on available to view and purchase in the gift shop.

Seasons/Hours: Year-round: 8 am–5 pm M–F; 1 pm–5 pm Sa & Su

Cost: Free

Address: 540 W Hills Crl., Owatonna, MN 55060

Write to: Owatonna Area Chamber of Commerce & Tourism, 320 Hoffman Dr, Owatonna, MN 55060

Phone: 507.451.7970 or 800.423.6466 for group tours

E-mail: museum@ci.owatonna.mn.us

Website: www.orphanagemuseum.com

Directions: From the S on I-35, take Exit 41 and go E on Bridge St. Turn left on State Ave to West Hills Crl. From the N on I-35, take Exit 42 and go E on Hoffman Dr. Turn right on State Ave to West Hills Crl.

STEELE COUNTY HISTORICAL SOCIETY

㉘ **Description:** Steele County Historical Society maintains a site called The Village of Yesteryear, which features 15 buildings dating as far back as the 1850s. Visitors can plan to spend 1½ hours on the tour which leads through the fire station, the blacksmith shop, general store, 1868 Dunnell Mansion, farm machinery building, the post office and many other buildings throughout the village.

Seasons/Hours: May–Sept 30: 1 pm–5 pm Tu–F; tours at 1:30 pm & 3:30 pm; or by appointment

Cost: Adults: $5, students: $2, children 12 and under: free

Address: 1448 Austin Rd., Owatonna, MN 55060

Phone: 507.451.1420

E-mail: schs@mnic.net

Website: www.owatonna.org/visit/interest/village.php

Directions:	From I-35 S, take Exit 40 E. Exit at the first Owatonna exit. Go to the stoplight and turn right on 18th St. Go to the 4-way stop, turn left on Austin Rd and go about ½ mi. Museum is on the left.

WEST CONCORD HISTORICAL MUSEUM

㉙ *Description:*	With a seashell collection and a plethora of themed rooms about everything from fashion to war vets, this museum is not to be missed, nor is the daily attic sale benefitting the Historical Society.
Seasons/Hours:	Year-round: 9 am–2 pm M, W–F; 2 pm–4 pm 1st Su of every month
Cost:	Free
Address:	500 6th St, West Concord, MN 55985
Phone:	507.527.2628
Website:	www.dodgecohistorical.addr.com/sites.htm
Directions:	From the Twin Cities, take Hwy 52 S to Hwy 56 into West Concord. Turn W on Irwin St and go to 6th St.

ARCHES MUSEUM OF PIONEER LIFE

㉚ *Description:*	With a passion for history and a love of children, the late Walter Rahn started this roadside museum to bring the history to the children. Collecting what he could and building what he could not find, Walter developed what lives today as a glimpse into the 1860s and beyond. It features a log home, country school and barn.
Seasons/Hours:	June–Aug: 1 pm–5 pm W–Su; or by appointment
Cost:	Adults: $3, students: $1; children under 6, members, and students doing research: free
Write to:	PO Box 33, Lewiston, MN 55952
Phone:	507.523.2111 or 507.454.2723
E-mail:	wchs@luminet.net
Website:	www.winona.msus.edu/historicalsociety/sites/arches.asp
Directions:	Located on Hwy 14 midway between Stockton and Lewiston. It is nine mi. W of Winona. Watch for signs.

BUNNELL HOUSE

㉛ Description: Granted permission by Chief Wapasha, area fur trader Willard Bunnell built this house on the Dakota land that is now the town of Homer. Visitors are guided through this rural Gothic-style house which still holds many mid- to late-1800s artifacts as a record of the history between the pioneers and the Native Americans.

Seasons/Hours: Memorial Day–Labor Day: 10 am–5 pm W–Sa; 1 pm–5 pm Su

Cost: Adults: $3, students: $1

Write to: 160 Johnson St, Winona, MN 55987

Phone: 507.452.7575 or 507.454.2723

Website: www.winona.msus.edu/historicalsociety/sites/

Directions: Homer is a small community a few mi. SE of Winona along Hwy 14/16. Watch for signs.

CHRISTIAN BUNGE, JR. STORE MUSEUM

㉜ Description: This stone building was built by Christian Krueger in 1890 and is now on the Register of Historic Places. It is made of solid stone quarried from Winnebago Valley, a few miles from Eitzen, and brought to the site to be fitted and placed. Krueger used no big machinery to raise the stones into place, and upon completion received $800 for his work. Today this museum holds a large collection of Native American artifacts and many antiques.

Seasons/Hours: June–Aug: 1:30 pm–4 pm Su; or by appointment

Cost: Donation

Address: Cty Rd 2 (Main St) and Iowa Ave, Eitzen, MN 55931

Write to: Houston County Historical Society, 104 History Ln, Caledonia, MN 55921

Phone: 507.725.3884

Directions: From Caledonia, head S on Hwy 44, then continue S on Hwy 76 to Eitzen.

CHURCH OF THE HOLY COMFORTER

㉝ *Description:* A visit to The Church of the Holy Comforter is an opportunity to step back in time and recapture the wholesome religious aspirations of the area's first settlers. Listed on the National Register of Historic Places, this is a prime example of "prairie architecture" and reflects the simplicity and pervasiveness of religion in the lives of its members. The church is available for weddings and other functions for a nominal fee.

Seasons/Hours: Year-round: open by appointment

Cost: Donations appreciated

Address: Main St (Cty Rd 3), Brownsville, MN

Mail to: Houston County Historical Society, 104 History Ln, Caledonia, MN 55921

Phone: 507.725.3884

E-mail: webmaster@brownsville.cc

Directions: From Hwy 14 S in La Crescent, continue going S on Hwy 16 then turn left and go S on Hwy 26 to Brownsville. From Caledonia, take Hwy 249 E to Hwy 26 and go N (left) to Brownsville. The church is on Main St (Cty Rd 3).

1877 PETERSON STATION MUSEUM

㉞ *Description:* The Peterson Railroad depot has been restored and moved from its original location near the old railway. This museum has one of the most complete collection of material relating to Peterson and the surrounding area. It consists of over 2,500 photographs, area business advertising items and memorabilia and family history research materials including obituaries.

Seasons/Hours: Memorial Day–Labor Day: 1 pm–4 pm M & Th; 11 am–4 pm Sa & Su; or by appointment

Cost: Donation

Address: 228 Mill St, PO Box 233, Peterson, MN 55962

Phone: 507.895.2551

E-mail: johdar@acegroup.cc

Directions: From Rochester, take I-90 E. From La Crosse, take I-90 W to the Rushford Exit. Turn left onto Hwy 43 and go ten mi. to Rushford. Turn right on Hwy 16 and go four mi. to Peterson's Mill St.

HOUSTON COUNTY HISTORICAL SOCIETY

㉟ Description: The society collects, preserves and tells the story of Houston County's past through museum exhibits, photographs, research materials, educational programs, tours and historic sites. Its extensive collection of research materials includes birth, death and marriage records, over 17,000 photographs and genealogies.

Seasons/Hours: Year-round: 10 am–4 pm M–W;
June–Sept: 1 pm–4 pm Sa–Su; or by appointment

Cost: Donation

Address: 104 History Ln., Caledonia, MN 55921

Phone: 507.725.3884

Website: www.lacrosselibrary.org/guide/houston.html

Directions: From Main St in Caledonia, go E to History Ln.

JULIUS C. WILKIE STEAMBOAT CENTER

㊱ Description: This full-scale steamboat replica is home to many river life artifacts, with many miniature boat models and an entire floor of exhibits dedicated to the Victorian era when steamboats reigned supreme.

Seasons/Hours: May–mid-Oct: 10 am–4 pm W–Su

Cost: Adults: $2, children 5–12: $1, children under 5: free

Address: Levee Park, PO Box 733, Winona, MN 55987

Phone: 507.454.1254

Directions: From Hwy 61, turn NE towards the river on Huff St, then right on Broadway, then left on Main St. The Steamboat Center is down on the bank of the Mississippi River at the end of Main

PICKWICK MILL

㊲ Description: Completed in 1858 with nails only in the floor, this mill operated for 120 years, producing as much as 18,600 pounds of flour a day during its heyday. Today, visitors can see the mill building repaired and restored to its original state. See the water wheel, millstones, and six floors of working machinery from the 120 years of milling history in Pickwick. Spend a day trout fishing, boating or swimming at Mill Pond, bring a picnic or eat at the restaurant with a view of the falls.

Seasons/Hours:	June–Aug: 10 am–5 pm Tu–Su; May, Sept and Oct: 10 am–5 pm Sa–Su
Cost:	Adults: $3, children grades K–8: $1, youth grades 9–12: $2; group rate: $2.50 per person; group drivers and teachers: free
Write to:	Pickwick Mill, Inc., Rt 4 Box 219, Winona, MN 55987-9436
Phone:	507.457.0499 or 507.452.9658
Directions:	Take Hwy 61 S to Cty Rd 7 and go S two mi. to Pickwick.

RUSHFORD AREA HISTORICAL SOCIETY DEPOT

㊳ *Description:*	The museum is located in a two-story Southern MN Railway Company Depot, still on its original site built in 1867. Additional RAHS buildings include a schoolhouse, chapel and old jail. The Museum has local and genealogical information for on-site research. The depot also serves as a DNR Trail Center, as it is located alongside the Root River Trail.
Seasons/Hours:	Oct–April: 8:30 am–4 pm M–F; May–Sept: 8:30 am–4 pm daily
Cost:	Free, donations appreciated
Address:	401 S Elm, PO Box 98, Rushford, MN 55971
Phone:	507.864.7560
E-mail:	spartz@acegroup.cc
Website:	www.rushfordmn.com/member_dir_attraction.shtml#rhd
Directions:	From I-90 via Hwy 43, Hwy 30 or Hwy 16, the museum is one block off all three highways on Elm St S.

SCHECH'S WATER MILL

㊴ *Description:*	This 1876 mill was once used to grind Schech's Best Flour. Schech's Water Mill still grinds feed for farm animals.
Seasons/Hours:	Year-round: Sa–Su by appointment, call ahead
Cost:	$3
Address:	12559 Mill Rd., Caledonia, MN 55921
Phone:	507.896.3481
Directions:	From Caledonia, go six mi. NW of Caledonia on Cty Rd 10.

WINONA COUNTY HISTORICAL SOCIETY MUSEUM

40 Description: Located in the former National Guard Armory, this museum is as unique as the town's history. Fascinating displays include stained glass windows, the city's early sewage system and the Armory's Cold War plans. The museum is home to an excellent gift shop and a nationally-renowned children's exhibit where visitors can explore a tipi, a cave and a river steamboat. Archives include documentation on genealogical and natural histories.

Seasons/Hours: Year-round: 9 am–5 pm M–F; 12 pm–4 pm Sa–Su; closed weekends in Jan and Feb

Cost: Adults: $3, students: $1; children 7 and under, members, and students doing research: free

Address: 160 Johnson St, Winona, MN 55987

Phone/Fax: Ph: 507.454.2723; Fax: 507.454.0006

E-mail: wchs@luminet.net

Website: www.winona.msus.edu/historicalsociety/

Directions: From Hwy 14/61, turn on Huff St and head NE to 4th St Turn right and go to Johnson St, then turn left. The museum is between 3rd and 4th St.

Don't miss this: The Historic Downtown Walking Tour—available from the Winona County Historical Society or the Winona CVB—is a brochure detailing a walking tour of historic Winona. The brochure notes 27 historic buildings and sites located in downtown in Winona.

Legend has it that a Dakota maiden by the name of Winona threw herself from a precipice on the shores of Lake Pepin rather than marry a man—chosen by her parents—that she did not love.

SOUTHEAST MINNESOTA FESTIVALS

LISTED ALPHABETICALLY

AUTUMN IN THE VILLAGE

Description:	Embrace autumn with the community of Albert Lea, celebrating with historical demonstrations, food, music and dancing.
Occurrence:	September
Write to:	Freeborn County Historical Museum, 1031 Bridge Ave, Albert Lea, MN 56007
Phone:	507.373.8003
E-mail:	fchm@smig.net
Directions:	From I-90, take Exit 157 and go two mi. S.

BIG ISLAND RENDEZVOUS

Description:	This is Minnesota's largest fur trade history event with over 1,000 costumed participants, 250 tents, colonial cuisine, colonial crafts and stage entertainment.
Occurrence:	First weekend in October
Write to:	Albert Lea/Freeborn Co. CVB, 143 W Clark, Albert Lea, MN 56007
Phone:	800.658.2526 or 507.373.3938
E-mail:	bigisland@albertlea.org
Website:	www.bigislandfestival.org
Directions:	Take I-90 Exit 157 (just W of I-35) and follow signs. After two stoplights the fair grounds are on the right-hand side.

BUFFALO BILL DAYS

Description:	There is a variety of entertainment possibilities for all ages. Volleyball and softball tournaments, beer and brat tents, food booths, flea markets, dances, kids' games and much more.
Occurrence:	First week in August
Phone:	507.467.2696 or 800.944.2670
E-mail:	lvc@acegroup.cc
Website:	www.lanesboro.com/lanesboro-calendar.html#august
Directions:	To event: from Rochester, take Hwy 52 S to Fountain City, then Hwy 8 E to Lanesboro.

 EDDIE COCHRAN DAYS

Description:	Eddie Cochran Days is a time to remember Eddie, a rock and roll artist whose life ended early, dear to many people. A car show, a cruise around the Fountain Lake and street dancing are just the beginning of a fun time. The Freeborn County Historical Museum has Eddie Cochran memorabilia on display for their visitors.
Occurrence:	Father's Day weekend
Write to:	Albert Lea/Freeborn Co. CVB, 143 W Clark, Albert Lea, MN 56007
Phone:	507.373.3938
Website:	www.smig.net/fchm/eddiecochran.htm
Directions:	To event: take Exit 11 off of I-35 to get to the Country Inn where many events take place. There are also events at the fair grounds off of Bridge St.

GRUMPY OLD MEN FESTIVAL

Description:	This annual celebration takes place where the movies were set. Bundle up and take part in the ice-fishing contest, a spaghetti feed, bowling, golf and an ice shack contest.
Occurrence:	Last Saturday in February
Cost:	Admission for the golf tournament and cover charges for bands.
Write to:	160 Main St, PO Box 105, Wabasha, MN 55981

Phone:	Ph: 651.565.4158 or 800.565.4158; Fax: 651.565.2808
E-mail:	info@wabashamn.org
Website:	www.wabashamn.org, click on "Event Calendar" then click to February and click on "Grumpy Festival."
Directions:	Wabasha is located at the intersection of Hwy 60 E and Hwy 61 along the Mississippi River.

HERITAGE CELEBRATION

Description:	Celebrating the diverse heritage found in Faribault, this festival includes a parade, art show, carnival, street dance, car show and a fishing contest.
Occurrence:	Second or third weekend in June
Write to:	530 Wilson Ave, Faribault, MN 55021
Phone/Fax:	Ph: 507.334.4381 or 800.658.2354; Fax: 507.334.1003
E-mail:	jeul@faribaultmn.org
Website:	www.faribaultmn.org/comm_fboevents.html
Directions:	From I-35, take the Faribault Exit 56 into Faribault. Events are happening throughout town.

HISTORICAL EXTRAVAGANZA

Description:	This annual event is held at the Village of Yesteryear and includes, basket-making, weaving, woodworking, food stands, a silent cake auction, crafts in the schoolhouse and many other activities.
Occurrence:	Second Sunday in July: 11 am–5 pm
Cost:	Adults: $3; children 12 and under: free
Write to:	1448 Austin Rd., Owatonna, MN 55060-4018
Phone/Fax:	Ph: 507.451.1420; Fax: 507.456.1220
E-mail:	schs@mnic.net
Website:	www.owatonna.org, click on "A Place to Visit," then scroll to "Calendar of Events"
Directions:	From I-35 S, take the first Owatonna exit. Go to the stoplight and turn right on 18th St. At the 4-way stop turn left on Austin Rd and go about ½ mi. The Village of Yesteryear is on the left.

 # INDEPENDENCE DAY

Description:	Come enjoy the fun and excitement of Independence Day in Forestville like so many did in 1899. The town provides political speeches by historical characters, music, contests, games and refreshments that are re-created to display what went on in the late 1890s.
Occurrence:	July 4th
Write to:	Rt 2, Box 128, Forestville State Park, Preston, MN 55965
Phone:	507.765.2785
E-mail:	forestville@mnhs.org
Directions:	Located in Forestville State Park on Hwy 16 between Preston and Spring Valley; 30 mi. S of Rochester.

 # MANTORVILLE MARIGOLD DAYS

Description:	Celebrate the marigold in Mantorville; see the 52K Stagecoach Run, Big Iron Classic Truck Show and Parade and Fiddler's Jamboree along with other music on-stage. Take part in the water fight or the co-ed softball tournament while the kids can enter the pedal tractor pull or fishing contest.
Occurrence:	First weekend in September
Write to:	Mantorville Chamber of Commerce, PO Box 358, Mantorville, MN 55955
Phone:	507.635.2331
Website:	www.mantorville.com/marigold/marigold.html
Directions:	From Hwy 52, take Hwy 14 to Kasson, then N on Hwy 57 to Mantorville.

 # RICE COUNTY FREE FAIR

Description:	This annual fair includes a plethora of things to do and see, including 4-H exhibits, a demolition derby, a truck pull, a motocross race and an animal show.
Occurrence:	Third week in July
Write to:	Box 393, Faribault, MN 55021
Phone/Fax:	Ph: 507.332.2470; Fax: 507.685.4256
E-mail:	jhermel@cvel.net

Website:	www.faribaultmn.org/comm_fboevents.html
Directions:	From Faribault, go N on Hwy 3 to the fairgrounds.

 **RIVER CITY DAYS**

Description:	Three days in August are filled with fun for all ages including activities such as music, crafts, dragon boat races, a parade, fireworks, a car show, tractor pull and lumberjack show.
Occurrence:	August
Write to:	Red Wing Visitors & Convention Bureau, 420 Levee Street, Red Wing, MN 55066
Phone:	651.385.5934 or 800.498.3444; Chamber of Commerce: 651.388.4719
E-mail:	info@redwing.org
Website:	www.redwing.org/calendars/aug.html
Directions:	From Hwy 61 in Red Wing, take Broad St, to Levee Rd to Bay Point Dr.

 **ROCHESTERFEST**

Description:	This annual city-wide celebration has a little something for everyone, including a lumberjack competition, street dance, treasure hunt, grand parade, live music and plenty of food.
Occurrence:	Typically starts on Father's Day and continues for the following nine days.
Write to:	Rochesterfest, PO Box 007, Rochester, MN 55903
Phone:	507.285.8769 or 800.634.8277
Website:	www.rochesterfest.com
Directions:	From Hwy 52 in Rochester, take E 2nd St SW to 1st Ave SW and go S. Go E on 4th St SW to 11th Ave S then go N to 2nd Ave.

 **STEAMBOAT DAYS**

Description:	Join this annual celebration of Winona's steamboat history with fireworks, a boat regatta, a parade, live music, a carnival, golf and softball tournaments and a beverage tent.
Seasons/Hours:	Third weekend in June

Phone:	507.452.2272 or 800.657.4972
E-mail:	jlacroix@rconnect.com
Website:	www.winonasteamboatdays.com
Directions:	From Hwy 61, turn NE towards the river on Huff St, then right on Broadway, then left on Main St. Levee Park is down on the bank of the Mississippi River at the end of Main.

STEELE COUNTY HISTORICAL SOCIETY CHRISTMAS IN THE VILLAGE

Description:	This annual event is held at the Village of Yesteryear and includes sleigh rides, music, the Dunnell Mansion completely decorated, a fancy cookie sale, visits with Santa and unique gift items in the Emporium Gift Shop.
Occurrence:	First weekend in December
Write to:	1448 Austin Rd., Owatonna, MN 55060
Phone/Fax:	Ph: 507.451.1420; Fax: 507.456.1220
E-mail:	schs@mnic.net
Directions:	From I-35 S, take Exit 40 to Hwy 14 E. Exit at the first Owatonna exit and go to the stoplight. Turn right on 18th St and go to the 4-way stop. Turn left on Austin Rd and go about 1/2 mi. The Village of Yesteryear is on the left.

WATER SKI DAYS

Description:	In honor of the invention of water skiing on Lake Pepin by Ralph Samuelson, Lake City hosts this three-day celebration which includes a water ski show, live music, a parade, carnival rides, crafts and a classic car show.
Occurrence:	Last weekend in June
Phone:	(877) 525.3248 or 651.345.4123
E-mail:	lcchambr@mr.net or tourism@lakecity.org
Website:	www.lakecity.org, click on "Calendar," then click on "June"
Directions:	65 mi. S of Mpls/St. Paul on Hwy 61. Events schedule available at the Chamber of Commerce, downtown on Washington St.

Description:	Chatfield hosts this annual Wild West celebration which includes a parade, carnival, horse show and craft show.
Seasons/Hours:	Second weekend in August
Phone:	507.867.3810
Website:	www.ci.chatfield.mn.us, click on "Community Events;" at bottom click on "See All Items" then on "Chatfield Western Days"
Directions:	20 mi. S of Rochester on Hwy 52.

COUNTIES INCLUDED IN THIS SECTION:

DODGE COUNTY was established in 1855. It was named for Henry Dodge, who at the time was governor of the Wisconsin Territory. The county seat is Mantorville. The area is 440 square miles, which ranks 79th in the state. Population is 17,731 people, which ranks 51st in Minnesota. Population density is 40.3 people per square mile, which ranks 32nd in the state.

FILLMORE COUNTY was established in 1853. It was named after President Millard Fillmore, who was president while Minnesota was being considered for statehood. The county seat is Preston. The area is 862 square miles which ranks 28th in the state. The population is 21,122 people, which ranks 46th in Minnesota. Population density is 24.5 people per square mile, which ranks 48th in the state.

FREEBORN COUNTY was established in 1855. It was named after William Freeborn who served as a territorial legislature member and mayor of Red Wing. The area is 723 square miles, which ranks 37th in the state. Population is 32,584 people, which ranks 29th in Minnesota. Population density is 46 people per square mile, which ranks 29th in the state.

GOODHUE COUNTY was established in 1853. It was named for James Madison Goodhue who was the first newspaper editor in Minnesota. The county seat is Red Wing. The area is 780 square miles, which ranks 30th in the state. Population is 44,127 people, which ranks 19th in Minnesota. Population density is 58.2 people per square mile, which ranks 21st in the state.

HOUSTON COUNTY was established in 1854. It was named for Sam Houston, who was President of Texas until it became part of the United States. The county seat is Caledonia. The area is 569 square miles, which ranks 62nd in the state. Population is 19,718 people, which ranks 48th in Minnesota. Population density is 35.3 people per square mile, which ranks 37th in the state.

MOWER COUNTY was established in 1855. It was named for John E. Mower who was a politician and territorial council member. The county seat is Austin. The area is 712 square miles, which ranks 46th in the state. Population is 38,603 people, which ranks 24th in Minnesota. Population density is 54.2 people per square mile, which ranks 24th in the state.

OLMSTED COUNTY was established in 1855. It was named for David Olmsted, the first mayor of St. Paul. The county seat is Rochester. The area is 564 square miles, which ranks 46th in the state. Population is 124,277 people, which ranks 8th in Minnesota. Population density is 190.3 people per square mile, which ranks 8th in the state.

RICE COUNTY was established in 1853. It was named for Henry Mower Rice, one of the first two senators in the state who was also involved as a fur agent. He aided in the negotiation of several treaties which called for lands to be ceded for settlement. The county seat is Faribault. The area is 516 square miles, which ranks 68th in the state. Population is 56,665 people, which ranks 14th in Minnesota. Population density is 113.9 people per square mile, which ranks 11th in the state.

STEELE COUNTY was established in 1855. It was named for Franklin Steele, a prominent governmental contractor and founding member of the Minnesota Historical Society. The county seat is Owatonna. The area is 440 square miles, which ranks 79th in the state. Population is 33,680 people, which ranks 27th in Minnesota. Population density is 78.4 people per square mile, which ranks 16th in the state.

WABASHA COUNTY was established in 1849. It was named for three generations of influential Dakota leaders. The name is derived from the Dakota word "wapashaw" which means "red leaf." The county seat is Wabasha. The area is 549 square miles, which ranks 63rd in the state. Population is 21,610 people, which ranks 45th in Minnesota. Population density is

41.2 people per square miles, which ranks 31st in the state.

WINONA COUNTY was established in 1854. It was named after the eldest daughter of Chief Wapasha. "Wenonah" is the Dakota Sioux word for "first born daughter." The county seat is Winona. The area is 642 square miles, which ranks 51st in the state. Population is 49,985 people, which ranks 18th in Minnesota. Population density is 79.8 people per square mile, which ranks 15th in the state.

Attractions by City

ATTRACTIONS BY COUNTY

ATTRACTIONS BY INTEREST

AGRICULTURE

FESTIVALS

EARLY INDUSTRY

HERITAGE GARDENS

FESTIVALS

MINNESOTA'S SIGNIFICANT PEOPLE

FESTIVALS

NATIVE AMERICAN

NATIONAL REGISTER OF HISTORIC PLACES

FESTIVALS

RAILROAD INTERESTS

SIGNIFICANT ARCHITECTURE

WALKING TOURS

ALPHABETICAL